*York is
Living History*

The Old Gaol as it looks today.

YORK IS LIVING HISTORY

Neil Rolde

HARPSWELL PRESS / BRUNSWICK, MAINE

To the People of the Town of York

Acknowledgments

A number of persons have helped me in preparing this book and an author, particularly one who is a politician, hesitates to name any for fear of leaving someone out. But I'll take the chance, because I do want to thank Betty Winton and Martha Gifford for their assistance at the Wilcox House Library, Linda Coburn for her assistance at the York Library, John Bardwell for reading the manuscript and other assistance, and to those who helped me gather material and who offered their collections of photographs, including Mrs. Leslie E. Freeman, Henry Cadwalader, Leo Blaisdell, Mrs. Dorothea Thompson, Mr. and Mrs. Arthur Best, Mr. and Mrs. Raymond Bone, Mr. and Mrs. Elwell Taplin, Alice Parsons and Joseph Parsons. I appreciate any and all help that I have received.

Copyright © 1975 by Neil Rolde.

All rights reserved. No part of this book may be reproduced or transmitted in any form or by any means, electronic or mechanical, including photocopying, recording or by any information storage and retrieval system, without permission in writing from the publisher.
Harpswell Press, Simpson's Point Road, Brunswick, Maine 04011
Library of Congress catalog card number: 74-28772
International Standard Book Number:
  0-88448-003-8 *paperbound*
  0-88448-004-6 *clothbound*
Designed by Wladislaw Finne
First edition
Printed in the United States of America

Contents

Acknowledgments iv
Foreword vi
Introductory Note vii
York, Maine 1
Sir Ferdinando Gorges 2
Massachusetts Takes Over 4
Early York in Literature 10
Hard Times, War, and Indians 13
The York Massacre 16
The Frontier Town 21
York Before the Revolution 28
War on Canada 30
Steps Toward the Revolution 33
The Revolution 39
A New Nation 46
A New State 49
Following Statehood 53
The Growth of Tourism 55
Separation Sentiment Starts 61
The Bridge 63
"Yorktown," "Gorges," and the Fight in the Legislature 66
The 250th Anniversary Celebration 70
Some Literary Allusions 74
In Conclusion 83

Foreword

Books, films, travel brochures, postcards, slides, and snapshots have captured the many sides of Old York as it has evolved from a fishing village to a resort community on the edge of megalopolis.

Sir Ferdinando Gorges called it "a faire towne," a travel columnist called it "a perfect place for a colonial muster," and the National Park Service called it "a sweeping panorama of one of the most historically significant areas in our nation."

Local preservationists and historians have worked hard to maintain the dignity and integrity of the community with its architectural treasures. The Old York Historical and Improvement Society and the Society for the Preservation of Historic Landmarks in York County are complemented by the colorful York Militia Company, which represents the state of Maine as the Governor's Ceremonial Footguards.

York is "living history." Most of the homes that are listed in the National Register of Historic Places are on the original foundations and have been carefully preserved by private owners. The Old Gaol, Jefferds Tavern, the Emerson-Wilcox House, the Marshall Store, the Hancock Warehouse, the Elizabeth Perkins House, and the Old Schoolhouse capture particular moments in history. Sewall's Bridge, the old burying ground, and Maud Muller Spring are unique landmarks that have been saved by people who cared. York Harbor Reading Room, York Country Club, and the First Parish Church attract photographers, writers, and historians.

York is living history because the sounds of flintlock muskets and colonial drummers are not out of place on the village green or on the lawns of Jefferds Tavern. A colonial church service, a militia ball, or a muster are so appropriate that the sight of men in Revolutionary War uniforms is to be expected. The sound of fife and drum music causes everyone to stand a little taller and reflect upon the American heritage.

Every local historian becomes enmeshed in the folklore of his community and hopes that others will share his enthusiasm. Unfortunately, many books on local history are large, heavy, and unnecessarily detailed. Neil Rolde has prepared this book to give the reader a complete picture of the history of this community but without the exhaustive detail that is of interest only to the scholar. Maybe he will capture your interest and you will become more involved with some aspect of the community's past. In Old York, it is very easy to become involved. That's why we say that York is living history.

John D. Bardwell
February 15, 1974

Introductory Note

For a vacationer or a visitor to a new place, there is barely time for a glimpse of the present scene, never mind an opportunity to learn the area's history. One enjoys the beauties and the pleasures the particular locale has to offer and then leaves, still a stranger.

To a degree, the same is often true for the town's inhabitants. Even of the community that is one's birthplace, so much is unknown, unexplored — and too often unappreciated.

It is for such reasons that this volume has been written. It is not a guidebook in the usual sense, but rather an attempt to impart some of the flavor, both past and present, of a particular town that has, as it happens, a degree of historical importance.

It is the author's hope that his work may contribute not only to the greater enjoyment of visitors and residents, but also to an increased understanding of our total American heritage.

York, Maine

York, an Atlantic seaboard village and resort, extends inland from the Maine coast along the the banks of the York and Cape Neddick rivers, reaching westward toward Mount Agamenticus into a region whose wilderness character is surprisingly well preserved. Like many another southern Maine community, it has areas that are neat, well kept, and scenically delightful — and it is a quiet place despite its growing population and the bustle of summer visitors.

With a permanent population that in 1973 was approaching 8,000 — a figure that expands to more than 20,000 during the summer — York is obviously no metropolis. Nor is it the scene of any cataclysmically important episode in the nation's past. The best it can offer in terms of a local battle is the violence of an Indian massacre during pre-Revolutionary times. But it is fascinating to speculate on what York might have become had it developed according to the abortive plans of a sixteenth- and early seventeenth-century British Cavalier, improbably named Sir Ferdinando Gorges (pronounced "gorgeous"), who may be considered its founder.

Sir Ferdinando came to establish York after many years of dabbling in plans for settlement in the New World. Granted a charter in 1635 to create his own proprietary province or "palatinate" of Maine, the English nobleman chose as the site of its capital a primitive fishing village identified on early maps under various names, including Agamenticus,[1] Bristol, and even Boston.[2] In the plans of Sir Ferdinando, his city, which he called Gorgeana, would rise to be a prosperous English county seat, complete with cathedral, market place, and annual trading fairs. Events were to rule out such a possibility. In 1652, the community was renamed the town of York. Through numerous vicissitudes, including attempts to divide it into several municipalities, Sir Ferdinando's settlement has remained the town of York to this day.

Sir William Pepperell, commander of the New England expedition to capture the French fortress of Louisbourg. This Kittery native was the first American to be knighted.

---

[1] Agamenticus was the original Abenaki Indian name given to the principal local river. "Aughemak-ti-kees," or "Snow-shoes River" was so named because of the shape of the pond from which it derived its source.

[2] In 1616, Captain Smith is said to have shown King Charles I, then Prince of Wales, a coastal map of the New World, on which the future Stuart King wrote "Boston" in place of "Agamenticus."

Sir Ferdinando Gorges

Sir Ferdinando Gorges had long held dreams of creating his own feudal empire in the unpopulated forests of North America. Despite his odd name, his British antecedents can be traced in a direct line back to the Norman Conquest and one Ralph de Gorges, who had left Normandy for England in 1066 along with William the Conqueror. As a member of the English landed nobility, Sir Ferdinando was well connected. He was related to Sir Walter Raleigh and Sir Humphrey Gilbert and he was also reputed to be a third cousin to Queen Elizabeth. But as a second son, unable to inherit his family's property, he was expected to make a name for himself on his own. We first hear of Sir Ferdinando as a captain in the British army fighting the Spaniards in the Lowlands. After being knighted on the battlefield, he was put in command of the fortress at Plymouth, a post he was to hold off and on for many years.

During the reign of Queen Elizabeth, hard times befell Sir Ferdinando. He was friendly with the Earl of Essex, who had procured him his knighthood and who was the queen's lover. In a mysterious episode, Essex was alleged to have conspired against the queen; he was beheaded, and Sir Ferdinando, who had tried to be an intermediary, spent a year in prison for his supposed complicity in the plot. With the advent of the first Stuart king, James I, Sir Ferdinando's fortunes improved. It was at this time that his interest in America began to be aroused.

In 1605, Sir Ferdinando participated in financing an expedition to the New World. Landing on the coast of Maine, the ship's captain, John Weymouth, kidnapped five Abenaki Indians and took them back to England, where they learned English. One of them was Squanto, who later befriended the Pilgrims. Three of these transplanted Americans stayed with Sir Ferdinando. Their tales of their native haunts — of the grandeur and resources of the vast, empty land they inhabited — changed the contemporary opinion that America was a narrow reef of rocks and mountains. They fired Sir Ferdinando with thoughts of monetary gain, and still more of power — for in his feudal world, land above all was *the* source of power.

Accordingly, in the following year, 1606, Sir Ferdinando and his friends formed a joint stock company to exploit the American continent. The company had two branches, one in London and one in Plymouth. It was the former, the Virginia Company, that settled Jamestown; the latter, the New England Company, after the failure in 1607 of its colony at Popham Beach, Maine, helped in the settlement of Massachusetts. Sir Ferdinando was also instrumental in forming the Council of New England, a body that theoretically had authority to rule over all settlements in the northern parts. This group was soon in conflict with John Winthrop and his fast developing Puritan commonwealth of Massachusetts Bay. By 1635, Sir Ferdinando's misgivings about these dissenting Puritans led him to found his palatinate once the Council of New England disbanded and he received sole jurisdiction over Maine. His choice of the palatinate form of government was deliberate because "palatinate" had a definite legal sense in feudal usage, wherein specific prerogatives were granted of an almost royal nature. Items normally reserved to the monarchy — for example, whales, sturgeons and treasure troves — went to the owner of a palatinate. Within his new possession, as lord proprietor, Gorges had quasi-absolute powers. He could appoint clergy, pardon offenders, proclaim martial law, keep a standing army, and govern pretty much howsoever he saw fit.

In setting up his capital of Gorgeana, Gorges also established the first chartered city among England's North American possessions. As incorporated in 1641, the city was to have a mayor, twelve aldermen, twenty-four councilmen, two courts and from two to four "sergeants of the white rod" to assist the mayor. Along with a corporate seal, this metropolis in embryo had the power to erect fortifications and was authorized to become the seat of a bishop of the Church of England. There was even a slight nod in the direction of democracy — a council to be elected by freeholders. To run things, Sir Ferdinando dispatched his nephew Thomas Gorges, with the title of "deputy governor and keeper of the provincial seal." Sir Ferdinando himself never set foot in his empire. The ship constructed to transport him there sank as it was being launched. This piece of bad luck was followed by worse ill fortune — the defeat of Charles I and his Cavalier armies in the English Civil War in 1646. A year later — before the executioner's axe ended the absolute rule of the second Stuart king, and with it the dream of a feudal empire in Maine — Sir Ferdinando himself was dead.

Massachusetts Takes Over

The community Gorges left behind at his death in 1647 had been in existence since 1630. Its earliest settler, Edward Godfrey, had been a prosperous London merchant when, at the age of 45, he had emigrated to America to start a new life. He was soon joined by Col. Walter Norton and Edward Johnson, both refugees from the stifling theological atmosphere of Puritan Massachusetts. Johnson's friend and neighbor Thomas Morton, founder of Merry Mount, a controversial colony near Quincy, Massachusetts, which the Puritans eventually closed down, likewise fled to York, to live out his days in more congenial surroundings.

Among other early arrivals were the progenitors of several families that are today prominent in York, including the first Blaisdell (Ralph), whose surname derived from Bleasdale Moors in northern Lancashire, and the first Bragdon (Arthur) from Stratford-on-Avon, where he was said to have been acquainted with William Shakespeare.

These beginning decades also witnessed the commencement of troubles with Indians. Col. Walter Norton and young John Godfrey, son of Edward, were both fatally tomahawked on a trading expedition to the Connecticut River in 1633. Violent death struck closer to home in 1644, with what appears to have been the town's first murder. The weighted body of Richard Cornish was found in the river, and his wife, a woman of bad reputation, was indicted, tried, convicted and executed for the crime — but not before she had accused the mayor of Gorgeana, Roger Garde, of having had illicit relations with her. Mayor Garde died shortly afterward, haunted by this aspersion on his honor and still more by the fact that it was believed. As one account puts it, he died crying out that the townspeople "had broke his hearte".

It had been to Roger Garde that Deputy Gov. Thomas Gorges entrusted affairs of state in 1643, when he left to fight on the side of the Parliament in the Civil War — for the younger Gorges, unlike his uncle, was sympathetic to the Puritan cause. The return of Thomas Gorges to England ended a period of relative stability for York, in which the deputy governor had displayed significant talent in guiding the primitive community. He dealt with difficult legal issues of land ownership and confronted and successfully weathered the challenge of a morally corrupt minister with strong political connections, Rev. George Burdett, who was ultimately convicted of adultery and other offenses prior to his being expelled from the colony. There was much to reform in early York. Sir Ferdinando's estates were in such bad condition that Thomas wrote a friend, "For me to undertake the repair of them would be to wash a blackamore," and he also wrote, "I found Sir Ferdinando's house much like your barn." A suggestion of his for increasing the economic potential of the settlement, but one which he never carried out, was to import into Maine Negro slaves and/or indentured poor children as cheap labor. Before leaving Gorgeana, Thomas entrusted his uncle's manor house, such as it was, to Mayor Garde. It remained without a caretaker following Garde's death and has long since vanished entirely. Even its location — rumored to have been at Point Christian on the York River — is no longer certain.

The departure of Thomas Gorges, the death of Sir Ferdinando, the triumph of Cromwell, and the execution of King Charles — these events all set the stage for a takeover by the rapidly growing Massachusetts Bay Colony (20,000 settlers between 1630 and 1640). The process began in 1651 when a commission was dispatched to subdue York's neighboring town of Kittery. This move was given force not only by the influence of a Puritan government in England, but also by veiled threats of armed invasion.

After Kittery gave in, fifty York residents signed a similar act of submission despite strong resistance by Edward Godfrey and others. Then, on December 8, 1652, a town meeting transformed the city of Gorgeana into the town of York, replacing the English pageantry of mayor and aldermen, sergeants of the white rod, and the entire government body of almost forty persons, with a board of five selectmen. The name of York was chosen to honor the recent surrender by the English city of the same name to the forces of Oliver Cromwell. (It is ironic that within a few decades an erstwhile Duke of York, the Stuart king James II, would be striving to destroy whatever independence Massachusetts had gained.)

Now that York had been annexed as a Massachusetts town, the land granted by the crown to Sir Ferdinando Gorges was divided among the citizens, since Massachusetts law held that towns possessed title to their own territory. Included among the awards of "common lands" to twenty-seven York freeholders were not only the Gorges lands but also those originally granted to Edward Godfrey. Under the new division, Godfrey was allowed to keep his own house lot of 35 acres, plus 500 acres of marsh along the river and 200 acres of upland. Yet, dissatisfied, he protested the disposition and sailed for England, there to plead his case in vain. Poor, stubborn Godfrey eventually died in debtor's prison.

Another development at about this time was the arrival in York of a dozen or so Highland Scots who had been taken prisoner by Cromwell at the battles of Dunbar and Worcester. The section of the town they first settled is known to this day as "Scotland." They came as indentured slaves, to be kept in servitude for six or seven years. Among the names bequeathed to York by this forced exile were those of Grant, Gowen, Junkins and McIntire. According to legend, Micum McIntire, the initial ancestor of the numerous York McIntires, had been picked at random to be shot, attempted to escape, and thereby so impressed his captors that they spared him. According to different sources, the story is strictly apochryphal.

At about this time, too, Edward Rishworth entered York's history. Unlike that of the McIntire family, the name of Rishworth is now entirely unknown in York or anywhere in the surrounding area. Rishworth was Recorder of the Province of Yorkshire (as Maine had been renamed) — a post that combined the duties of town and county clerk — and much more besides. Throughout a career that spanned forty years of the seventeenth century, he occupied a central position in the affairs of his community, always alert to the periodic necessity of walking a political tight-rope between warring factions.

Like many an able bureaucrat, Rishworth hung onto his job through competent work plus some encouragement of the belief that he was virtually indispensable — which indeed he was whenever there were deeds to be drawn, legalities to be recorded or papers of any sort to be put in order. The number of political pitfalls he managed to surmount is suggested by the following milestones: in 1652 he went to work under the government of Massachusetts; in 1665 he was employed by the Royal Commissioners who had superseded the government of Massachusetts; in 1668, when Massachusetts regained control, Rishworth was fired, to be reinstated through popular election following a public apology to the Bay Colony. In 1686 the government changed once again, with the appointment by James II of Sir Edmund Andros to rule New England — and once again Rishworth was out. Predictably enough, popular outcry brought him back as Deputy Recorder.

In 1688 or 1689 Rishworth died, not long before the arbitrary royalist rule of Andros was overthrown, bringing to a climax in the New World the struggle of the Puritans against the Stuarts, which had gone on for nearly half a century. That struggle left its indelible mark on the history of York, and is worth retracing in some detail.

The brief, three-year return to York (1665-1668) of a direct royal government, after thirteen years of Massachusetts rule, was mainly instigated by one Samuel Maverick[3] of Noddle Island, Boston Harbor. A settler who had arrived in Boston six years before John Winthrop and who was a continual thorn in the side of the saintly Puritan establishment, Maverick was the reputed originator of the triangular pattern involving Boston, the West Indies, and Europe in such ungodly trade commodities as rum and slaves. He also speculated in real estate and had acquired valuable property in York. When Massachusetts assumed control of York, Maverick lost his land.

In 1660 the Restoration that put King Charles II on the throne gave Maverick his opportunity for redress. His petitions, messages, and tireless lobbying brought about an investigation of the Bay Colony's usurpation of the Province of Maine. A royal commission was appointed and Maverick was named a commissioner. In his efforts Maverick had the backing of young Ferdinando Gorges, the founder's grandson, who was trying to recover a few lost lands of his own.

The leaders of the royal commission, Sir Robert Carr and Richard Nicolls, embarked for America accompanied by four hundred soldiers. They brought with them an

---

[3] Not to be confused with Samuel A. Maverick (1803-1870), to whom the origin of the word "maverick" has been traced, described as a "Texas pioneer who did not brand his cattle."

official letter declaring that in the opinion of the attorney general the take-over of Maine by Massachusetts had been illegal and ordering that authority be restored to Ferdinando Gorges. For all its physical and moral force, the commission argued fruitlessly with the Puritan officials in Boston. Proceeding to York, they were welcomed enthusiastically and the king's rule was immediately reestablished with the appointment of eleven royal justices. His mission seemingly fulfilled, Sir Robert Carr returned to England to report to the king. He died the day after he landed.

The "Merry Monarch," Charles II, was not greatly concerned with squabbles in the wilderness three thousand miles from London. The Boston Puritans, who *were* concerned, could wait to seize the initiative.

And although the royal commission had been welcomed, that sentiment was by no means unanimous. Thirteen years of Massachusetts rule had brought in new blood. An example was Nathaniel Masterson, who had close connections with the Pilgrims. Born at Leiden during the Pilgrim exile in Holland, he had been brought to Plymouth Plantation as a year-old baby. In York, as a partisan of Massachusetts, he held the office of Marshall of the Province, a position he lost in 1665 but regained in 1668. He was finally to be killed by Indians in the massacre of 1692.

Another eventual victim of the same massacre was Peter Weare, Massachusetts-born and the progenitor of a well-known family in present-day York. In 1652, when the Bay Colony took over, Weare received one hundred acres of land in York, and became a selectman and town clerk. During the Restoration period, he was the prime agitator for the return of York to Massachusetts rule. His trouble-making landed him in the town's newly built jail (which, now restored as the Old Gaol, is the earliest English government building left standing in the United States). Here, as Weare put it, "I found nothing but ye flore to ly upon." The jailer took pity on Weare and removed him to his own home. Weare's fellow citizens sent a petition to Massachusetts demanding his release and before long Massachusetts troops were sent to attend to just that.

Before going on to the somewhat comic-opera episode of the Massachusetts "invasion," it is appropriate to mention one particular signer of the Weare petition. This is Thomas Moulton, who came from a family of well-to-do yeomen in the English county of Norfolk. Their Norman ancestor, surnamed de Multon, was yet another who had arrived in England with William the Conqueror, and the Moultons of present-day York, its most numerous family, are all lineal descendants of Thomas. As an average citizen of his time, he was neither a strong partisan of Massachusetts — despite his signature on the petition to free Weare — nor strongly in favor of the crown.

Thus, like many of his fellow citizens, Moulton must have listened with something like an open mind to the proceedings that took place in July 1668, when a Massachusetts officer, Maj. Gen. John Leverett, rode into York, followed by twelve armed men on horseback. With swords drawn and drums beating, they advanced to the meetinghouse on Lindsay Road, where the inhabitants gathered for prolonged and heated discussion. Despite protests by the royal justices, the Massachusetts troopers proceeded to organize a new government. After three days, swords were sheathed. In England, King Charles was too busy with other matters to initiate any countermove.

But the bloodless coup in Maine did not end the problems of Massachusetts with the royal government. And in 1685, tyrannical James II succeeded his easygoing brother.

In the New World, James's mandate was carried out by his appointed governor, Sir Edmund Andros. Civil liberties were done away with; the charters of Massachusetts and other colonies were set aside; and Andros ruled a "Dominion of New England," extending from Maine to Delaware, without an elected assembly, strictly enforcing the oppressive English laws of trade and even attempting to supplant the Puritans' Congregational religion with High Church Anglicanism.

On April 18, 1689, eighty-six years almost to the day before the onset of the American Revolution, a portent of events to come exploded in the streets of Boston. Upon learning of the overthrow of James II by William of Orange, armed mobs surged through the Hub. Local patriots captured the commander of his Majesty's frigate, arrested Andros, clapped a pistol to the forehead of an Andros henchman — the obnoxious, fortune-seeking civil servant Edward Randolph — and induced him to call upon the city's garrison to surrender, which it did.

In the mini-revolution of 1689 was the germ of what was to happen later. The rebel Bostonians of 1689 even formed a "Committee of Safety" as a step toward restoring their old semi-independent government. Andros and Randolph were shipped back to England. The charter was restored. Regarding Maine, the government of the Bay Colony ended all dispute by purchasing the entire claim of Sir Ferdinando Gorges' heirs, at the bargain price of £1,250. What had been York, Maine, was now York, Massachusetts, presumably forever. Massachusetts seemed destined to remain forever a possession of England, loyal to the Protestant monarchs who had replaced James II in the revolution of 1688. With William and Mary on the throne, the epic struggle between Puritan and Cavalier had come to a peaceful conclusion, and the prolonged division between these different factions in the English-speaking world had ostensibly been healed.

Early York in Literature

But such difference of attitude between the two types of Englishmen had gone too deep to be wiped out by a political compromise — just how deep, no one has shown more clearly than that incomparable New England writer, Nathaniel Hawthorne. Among his tales there is one that, although not directly concerned with York, vividly summons an image of what life must have been like in the days we have been discussing. Entitled "The Maypole of Merry Mount," it depicts the colony founded by Thomas Morton, who has already been mentioned as having taken refuge at York after the Puritans closed his establishment down.

"Bright were the days at Merry Mount, when the Maypole was the banner staff of that gay colony!" Hawthorne begins his story,

> All the hereditary pastimes of Old England were transplanted hither. The King of Christmas was duly crowned, and the Lord of Misrule bore potent sway. On the eve of St. John, they felled whole acres of the forest to make bonfires, and danced by the blaze all night, crowned with garlands and throwing flowers into

the flame. At harvest time, though their crop was of the smallest, they made an image with the sheaves of Indian corn, and wreathed it with autumnal garlands, and bore it home triumphantly. But what chiefly characterized the colonists of Merry Mount was their veneration for the Maypole . . .

Its votaries danced round it, once, at least, in every month; sometimes they called it their religion, or their altar; but always, it was the banner staff of Merry Mount.

But nearby was another temperament, a life style that was the opposite side of the coin.

Unfortunately, there were men in the new world of a sterner faith than these Maypole worshippers. Not far from Merry Mount was a settlement of Puritans, most dismal wretches, who said their prayers before daylight, and then wrought in the forest or the cornfield till evening made it prayer time again. Their weapons were always at hand to shoot down the straggling savage. When they met in conclave, it was never to keep up the old English mirth, but to hear sermons three hours long, or to proclaim bounties on the heads of wolves and the scalps of Indians. Their festivals were fast days, and their chief pastime the singing of psalms. Woe to the youth or maiden who did but dream of a dance! The selectmen nodded to the constable; and there sat the light-heeled reprobate in the stocks; or if he danced, it was round the whipping-post, which might be termed the Puritan Maypole.

The story goes on to describe a raid upon the colony by the grim Puritan leader Endicott, his slashing down of the Maypole and the subjugation of those who, not as fortunate as Thomas Morton, could not escape to a place like York.

Hawthorne wrote, concluding on a dark note, "As the moral gloom of the world overpowers all systematic gayety, even so was their home of wild mirth made desolate amid the sad forest."

In another story, "The Minister's Black Veil," which is directly related to York, he picked up the same thread. Hawthorne, in a footnote, explicitly stated the source of his inspiration:

Here lyes buried the Body
of the Reverend
SAMUEL MOODY A.M.
The Zealous, faithful & successful
Pastor of the First Church of
CHRIST in YORK, was born in
NEWBURY JAN.ʸ 4. 1675.
graduated 1697; came hither
in MAY 1698, ordained in
DECEMBER 1700 & died here
Nov.ʳ 13. 1747.
For his further Character you
may read 2 Cor. 3. the Six first Verses.

Gravestone in York of the venerable "Father" Samuel Moody, who was pastor of York's First Congregational Church for nearly a half-century. Some credit Moody with having converted York from a relatively irreligious northern frontier town to a God-fearing Puritan community.

Another clergyman in New England, Mr. Joseph Moody,[4] of York, Maine, who died about eighty years since, made himself remarkable by the same eccentricity that is here related of the Reverend Mr. Hooper. In his case, however, the symbol had a different import. In early life he had accidently killed a beloved friend; and from that day till the hour of his own death, he hid his face from men.

In real life, the clergyman was locally famous as "Handkerchief Moody." He was the son of a still more famous pastor and spiritual leader, "Father" Samuel Moody, who served as a Congregational minister in York from 1698 to 1747. In Hawthorne's parable, Pastor Hooper one day simply dons a black veil and never takes it off again, although this act costs him his marriage and makes him a lonely object of mystification and awe among his parishioners. He cuts himself off entirely from the warmth of human contact for no obviously explainable reason. What the story expresses is possibly Hawthorne's conception of the New England Puritan character then being forged in small villages such as York. A pessimistic reflection of the harshness — moral as well as physical — of Puritan New England, the story ends:

> "Still veiled, they laid him in his coffin, and a veiled corpse they bore him to the grave. The grass of many years has sprung up and withered on that grave, the burial stone is moss-grown, and good Mr. Hooper's face is dust; but awful is still the thought that it mouldered beneath the Black veil."

Hard Times, War, and Indians

From 1689 onward, Massachusetts and Maine would be looked upon as outposts of English civilization — soon to face the onslaught of another imperial power, the France of Louis XIV, in alliance with the Abenaki Indian tribes whose lands the English had occupied.

[4] According to Edward W. Marshall in *Old York, Proud Symbol of Colonial Maine,* Moody was the great uncle of Ralph Waldo Emerson and it is conjectured that Hawthorne originally heard of the story of the veil through his friend, the Sage of Concord.

Headquartered in his chateau at Quebec City, Louis de Buade, Comte de Frontenac, the royal governor of New France, made a fitting representative of that power. He was, indeed, only slightly less impressive a personage than the king himself. It was said in France that Frontenac had been relegated to a colonial backwater instead of achieving a truly high position as a revenge for his formerly having been the lover of Madame de Montespan, the king's favorite mistress. What kept the count in his position, rumor also had it, was the influence of his estranged countess, Anne de la Grange-Trianon, who exercised her influence at court as the leader of a brilliant Parisian salon and was happy to help see to it that her husband stayed far away.

To the job of governing France's North American possessions, Frontenac brought dignity, ambition and energy. He was an elegant man, fastidious in dress. Willa Cather wrote of him in her novel, *Shadows On The Rock,* that "nothing annoyed him so much as his agent's neglecting to send him his supply of lavender water by the first boat in the spring. It vexed him more than a sharp letter from the Minister or even from the King." Yet Frontenac, even at an advanced age, is known to have danced by bonfires with half-naked Iroquois, and to have traveled hundreds of miles through the wilderness on Indian campaigns. He was also an implacable foe of all English settlers, ceaselessly imploring his sovereign for enough resources to drive the heretic Protestants into the sea. Always inadequately supplied and undermanned, he was forced to make heavy use of his Indian allies, most particularly the Abenakis, who had been converted, encouraged, and even sometimes led in their forays by missionaries from the Jesuit and other Catholic orders.

Fighting in these wars that broke in incessant waves over the northern countryside took a heavy toll in York, which remained a garrison town for nearly a century.

Several "garrison" houses, where settlers huddled to stave off Indian attacks, still stand today. One is the McIntire Garrison on Route 91 in York; another, the Frost Garrison, just over the town line in Eliot, still shows the indented marks of Indian arrows on its wooden outer walls. Both buildings are on the National Register of Historic Places.

Actually, however, York's problems with Indians cannot be attributed entirely to France's imperialistic designs. Hawthorne's description of the Puritans as having their weapons "always at hand to shoot down the straggling savage" or ready "to proclaim bounties on the heads of wolves and the scalps of Indians" points unmistakably to attitudes that couldn't help but lead to conflict. The Indians were steadily being deprived of their ancestral lands. They felt increasingly outnumbered, increasingly threatened. In June 1675, after three Wampanoag Indians were hanged at Plymouth, Massachusetts for murdering a converted Christian Indian named John Sassamon whom they suspected of serving as an informer for the English, King Philip's War broke out. All New England quickly blazed.

Until then, York had been spared any great amount of friction with the Indians. Although the site of the town had originally been an Indian settlement, an unidentified epidemic disease in 1616 had ravaged the local tribe, who had abandoned the area before the first whites had arrived.

The Indians of Maine were exclusively Algonquian-speaking, and are loosely identified as Abenakis. Of the two tribes remaining in Maine, the Penobscots and the Passamaquoddies, the language of the former has almost died out, whereas the Passamaquoddy language is still spoken. Closely related tribes are the Micmacs and the Malecites of Canada, now found mostly in the Province of New Brunswick.

The Mount Agamenticus of today was originally named by the Indians after Sasanoa, a notable chieftain who had been killed in 1607 fighting against the Micmacs. Following the disastrous epidemic of 1616, Sasanoa's people departed, leaving only place names behind them. Later there arose the curious legend of "Saint Aspinquid," an Indian convert to Christianity who died in 1682 and was supposedly buried with elaborate ceremony, including the sacrifice of some 6,721 animals, atop Mount Agamenticus.

There have been those in York who accepted the story of St. Aspinquid as true and who have gone so far as to search for his gravesite on the mountain and to give his name to the local Masonic Lodge. Others have maintained that the legend of St. Aspinquid more properly belongs to Nova Scotia, where "Saint Aspinquid Day" was regularly celebrated from 1774 to 1786. The demise of the custom reputedly occurred when certain residents of Halifax in a state of super-jollity celebrated by hauling down the British flag and replacing it with the stars and stripes — thus bringing wrath upon Saint Aspinquid in that staunchly Loyalist and anti-American province.

In York, the Indians made their first assault on September 25, 1675, three months after the start of King Philip's War. Seven people in the Cape Neddick region were killed and horrible atrocities were committed. One family, the Jacksons, was entirely wiped out.

The death of King Philip on August 12, 1676, and the signing of a treaty with the Abenaki leader Madockawando, on November 6, 1676, did not bring peace. On April 7, 1677, seven men were killed in the fields outside York as they prepared the ground for planting. Five days later two men, a woman and four children were butchered and two houses burned to the ground. Once again a treaty of peace was signed, on April 12, 1678, bringing an official end to what would be known as the first Indian War.

The second Indian War had wider ramifications. In part, the declaration of war against England by his Catholic Majesty Louis XIV had been in the hope of restoring James II, as a Roman Catholic sympathizer, to the English throne. In Quebec, Frontenac took up the challenge with his customary energy, gaining a psychological victory in 1690, when he repulsed an attack on Quebec City by Sir William Phips, a Maine-born adventurer, who had already made his fortune through the discovery of a fabulous sunken treasure in the West Indies. The response to Phips's ill-conceived adventure was a French counterattack throughout New England. In August 1690, a man was killed and a woman taken prisoner at York. In October, five citizens of York were killed. In the following year, a group of York inhabitants were set upon as they loaded a sloop; one was killed and nine wounded. Then, in 1692, came the massacre.

The York Massacre

Reports of massacres, whenever they occur, convey the same stunning sense of confusion and terror, and of individual histories; how this one escaped, how that one was killed. There is the grim counting up of casualties afterward. Yet it is always difficult, no matter how lurid the descriptions of what happened, to summon up fully the horror of sudden death visited upon an innocent community.

The Abenakis struck on Monday, January 25, 1692, in broad daylight. The day before had been a religious holiday, the Feast of the Purification of the Virgin Mary, known to the English as Candlemas.

Leading the attack by a band of approximately 150 warriors was Madockawando, the Abenaki chief. No Frenchman took part, but that the action was considered an arm of the French offensive against the English is clear from a report on the massacre by Monsieur de Champigny, the Intendant of Quebec, in which these Indians were called *"nos gens* - our people." Cotton Mather, the famous Puritan divine, described them as "Popish Indians."

All night, Madockawando and his subchieftains, Edegeremet and Moxis, waited huddled with their warriors at the foot of Mount Agamenticus. In the morning, it began to snow and there was some doubt about whether to go ahead with their plans. But the men were hungry. Thoughts of food and the booty they would find in the community below encouraged them to proceed.

Their first captive was a young lad, Arthur Bragdon, whom they found setting traps. Two other trappers who subsequently fell into their hands were massacred on the spot, but the Indians tied up Bragdon and held him prisoner.[5]

They then divided into two bands, one to assault the garrisons, the other to attack the people in their homes. Legend has it that before proceeding to the attack, some of the Indians piled their snowshoes by a certain boulder — which, needless to say, has been dubbed "Snowshoe Rock." It can be found today, duly marked with a plaque, alongside Chase's Pond Road.

Shortly after noon, the Reverend Shubael Dummer became a victim of the massacre. "As he was fleeing," according to Champigny, "he was brought down by a pistol shot while trying to escape on his horse." The murder of a minister of the gospel was seen as an act of particular

---

[5] What happened to Arthur Bragdon is not known. It is generally believed that he was released and lived through still other Indian raids.

frightfulness, one that would linger in the consciousness of New Englanders for years to come. Cotton Mather, in writing of it, expressed the full force of his outrage in almost biblical tones:

> Those bloodhounds, being set on by some Romish missionaries, had long been wishing they might embrue their hands in the blood of some New England minister and in this action they had their diabolical satisfaction. They left him dead among the tribe of Abel on the ground.

It is also reported that one Indian, having stripped the Reverend Mr. Dummer's body of its clerical robes, paraded in them before the dazed captives, taunting these unfortunates, who were soon to be taken to Canada, by delivering the parody of a sermon. The pastor's wife was exempted as a captive because of her age. But since her son had been taken prisoner, she insisted on traveling to Canada along with him. During the forced march, her son died. Her death, *"de chagrin* — of grief", as Champigny noted in his report, followed soon after her captors reached their Canadian base at Sillery just outside Quebec City.

At York the massacre went on for several hours as Indians roamed through the town, killing, looting, burning. The garrisons were not captured, or even seriously besieged. The savages were, as usual, capricious in their behavior. For example, four-year-old Jeremiah Moulton, after having witnessed the killing and scalping of his mother and father, was herded among the prisoners, but kept up such a show of resistance, continually screaming, struggling, and kicking, that the Indians, who admire bravery, reacted with amusement instead of using a tomahawk to smash his small head. When Jeremiah suddenly broke and ran, the Indians roared with laughter at the sight of his chubby legs churning through the snow, and finally let him escape. They and their descendants were to rue their leniency when Jeremiah Moulton, grown to manhood, became one of the fiercest Indian fighters in the history of New England.

Generally, the Indians chose their captives from among the young, especially young females. For one thing, children were easier to ransom for hard cash. For another, there were, no doubt, some instructions from the Jesuits, who saw girls as likely converts, who could then be expected to intermarry with the French. This is what happened to several of the York captives. Five-year-old Mary Austin, who on reaching Canada was sent to Montreal, was brought up in the Roman Catholic faith and married in 1710 to a carpenter named La Valterre, becoming the mother of nine French Canadians.

Even more interesting is the tale of the Sayward sisters. Mary Sayward, at the age of eleven, along with her younger sister, Esther, was brought to Montreal to be educated by the Sisters of the Congregation. She eventually took her vows as a member of the order, became Sister Marie-des-Anges and served as Mother Superior in several convents. Esther, on the other hand, married a wealthy merchant, Pierre de Lestage, who owned several estates. After her husband's death, Mme. de Lestage purchased a house adjoining the convent in which she had been educated, and gave generously to the support of the order. She was also a benefactress of the Ursuline convent in Quebec, where the former Esther Wheelwright, of Wells, another English captive and cousin of the Saywards, was mother superior.

In 1725, years after the massacre, Mme. de Lestage made a journey to York for a visit to her mother. This lady, Mary Plaisted, the daughter of Edward Rishworth, the long-time York officeholder, had three times been widowed and remarried, and had given birth to a son three weeks before the massacre. Herded toward Canada along with the other captives, she had trouble keeping up. An Indian finally killed her infant. Unlike her two daughters, she did not remain in Canada. Following her return from Canada as a redeemed prisoner, she lost still another daughter when ten-year-old Olive Plaisted was kidnapped by savages. Concerning the reunion with Esther in later years, it is touching to imagine the scene as that French-speaking lady, who by then probably spoke no other language, met with her sixty-five-year-old Yankee mother, who was probably no less ignorant of French. Afterward, Mary Plaisted lived on for thirty years more, to become the grand old lady of York.

Following their departure from York (carrying with them stores of powder plus lead obtained by smashing window panes and melting pewter), the Indians encamped

The McIntire Garrison before 1900.

for a night at Cape Neddick. The next day, as they marched through nearby Wells, they sent word to York of their willingness to redeem captives for a price.

In York a committee was formed, and collections were taken in churches throughout Massachusetts. By means of these funds and of others offered by private individuals, some thirty-six captives appear to have been ransomed after the Indians reached Sagadahoc, near what is now Bath, Maine. The rest of those redeemed came back in 1695 and 1698.

Meanwhile, Capt. John Floyd of Portsmouth, who commanded the troops that rushed to the relief of York, continued in pursuit until the deep snow compelled him to abandon the chase. There was nothing to be done now but bury the dead, add to York's defensive force, rebuild and carry on the life of the embattled community. In April 1692, two companies of soldiers arrived to relieve Floyd's troops and formed a permanent garrison. In the following year, nevertheless, a twelve-year-old boy, Charles Trafton, was captured and taken to Quebec, where he was rechristened Louis Marie Trafton. After serving for a time in Comte de Frontenac's retinue, Trafton eventually returned to York.

The Indian attacks continued. Vigilance had to be unremitting.

The Frontier Town

Not only was York physically a garrison town, but in 1699 an act of the Massachusetts Legislature (known then and to this day as the General Court) sealed this status into law. Entitled "An Act to Prevent the Deserting of the Frontier," it named eleven towns, including York, and stated that these communities should not "be broken up or voluntarily deserted," except by permission of the governor and council. Moreover, no inhabitant owning land in these communities could, unless given permission, "remove from thence with intent to sojourn or inhabit elsewhere." The penalty was forfeiture of all lands, which were then to be auctioned, the proceeds going for the common defense. A person allowed to leave who was capable of soldiering had to provide a substitute under penalty of a fine or "gaol." Under an amended version, anyone without land who left had to pay £10.

Today such legislation would surely be unconstitutional. But at the time, almost a hundred years before the existence of either the Constitution or Supreme Court, the frontier settlers had no choice but to provide Boston's first line of defense, largely at their own expense and even at the cost of their own lives. There were occasional shipments of food from outside sympathizers. Judge Samuel Sewall wrote in 1697, "I have once more the pleasure of sending a little corn to the poor families of York that are in distress, the Connecticut Gentlemen having consigned their contribution to me." The Province of Massachusetts was presumably paying for the soldiers it sent to York. Yet for the most part, Massachusetts did not do as much for its frontier communities as those communities were expected to do themselves.

From a broader viewpoint, York was the northern anchor of a thin line of English settlements that straggled down almost the length of the Atlantic Seaboard. Samuel Eliot Morison in his *Oxford History of the American People* describes this fifty-mile-wide fringe of habitations as "fairly continuous from York, Maine to Albemarle Sound, North Carolina." Then it skipped past 250 miles of Indian territory and reached South Carolina.

From 1698 onward, conditions around York were in constant flux; peace for a few years, then war, then peace again, but only briefly. There was the third Indian War, the fourth, and then the fifth. Madockawando had died in 1698. In 1702, Queen Anne renewed war against France. In York, Indian raids, deaths, and kidnappings continued for more than a decade.

The violence wasn't completely one-sided. In 1711, the townspeople captured three Indians and a Frenchman who had stolen a sloop in York Harbor. A summary court martial was held at the house of Samuel Donnell, a descendant of Henry Donnell, a fisherman, whose name is another prevalent one in York today. There is no record of what happened to the Frenchman, but the three Indians were marched out and hanged (probably at nearby Stage Neck, where this sort of thing took place) and their bodies were thrown into the sea. Their scalps, it should be added, were forwarded to Boston to substantiate a claim for bounty payments. Indian scalps were then worth £40 each. In 1973, during a debate in the Maine Legislature on animal bounties, it was suggested that the only bounty ever to be wholly successful in the Pine Tree State was that once put on Indian hair, a doleful observation no one could contest.

But to a settler under the intense psychic strain of staying ever alert and of having to witness hideous atrocities, an Indian was hardly human. He was simply a most dangerous and horrifying animal.

Complete revenge for the massacre was a decade in coming. But when York paid back the enemy in kind, the transaction was brutally thorough. It was with a celebrated episode in the struggle between France and England, the raid on Norridgewock.

Norridgewock, probably the largest permanent Indian camp in Maine, was also the site of a Roman Catholic church built by Père Sebastian Rasle, a Jesuit missionary. A monument near Skowhegan, in Somerset County, Maine, today marks the scene of his martyrdom. Accounted by some to have been a vicious, warmongering Indian commander, he was revered by others as saintly, intelligent, virtuous, and beloved.

The influence of the French missionaries over their native wards may be explained as stemming from an affinity of temperament and in the appeal to the Indians, in their relative unsophistication, of the elaborate and colorful ritual of the Roman Catholic Church. It has been said that the Indians could appreciate the symbolism of the Mass, since it conformed to their traditional conception of spiritual matters, which were likewise expressed in symbols — whereas the dry and solemn disquisitions by Puritan clergymen concerning such matters as atonement and justification by faith left the Indians unmoved. Even more persuasive was the willingness of the French to live among the Indians and learn their language. The French missionaries were not remote, but offered human warmth and companionship to the Indians, and thus gained their trust and devotion.

The same influence continues today among the Indians of Maine, the vast majority of whom are Roman Catholic. Even though education on the two Passamaquoddy reservations is paid for by the State of Maine, nuns do the teaching, an arrangement that has managed to surmount constitutional hurdles.

The mistakes made by the English in dealing with the Indians have been aptly described in an essay on Father

Rasle by the distinguished American poet, William Carlos Williams, from the collection entitled *In the American Grain*. He pictures the scene as Indian captives are brought before a noted Puritan religious leader, who attempts to disabuse them of the notions they have been taught by the French, including the need for the act of confession, and how he initially wins them over by his arguments.

> The Indians, in a rapture of admiration and surprise, to find one who had put them in the way of obtaining 'pardon for their sins' without paying beaver skins for it, fell on their knees, and, taking the minister's hand in theirs, began to kiss it in an extreme show of affection. But he shook them off with marked dislike of their posture.
> He would not suffer the contrite Indians to lay their hands upon him as the Catholic fathers in the north had done, but drew back and told them to address themselves to God alone.

Père Sebastian Rasle would not have acted like that. He had lived with his Indians for thirty-four years, as Williams says, "*TOUCHING* them every day." Père Rasle himself is described as:

> a spirit, rich, blossoming, generous, able to give and to receive, full of taste, a nose, a tongue, a laugh, enduring, self-forgetful in beneficence — a new spirit in the New World.

His life with the Indians was a continual adventure. Once Rasle would have been captured by the English had not two of his young warriors whisked him away in the middle of the night. It was winter, they had no provisions and the safety of Norridgewock was days away. They killed and ate a dog they had brought with them, along with "rock tripe" — the meager vegetation they scraped off boulders — and a certain kind of wood which they cooked until it was soft in the center. As they crossed a lake that had begun to thaw, the mushy ice gave way under their snowshoes. Rasle went in up to his knees, and one of his companions went in to his hips. Somehow, they helped each other get through.

Each spring the Indians would head for the seashore, where there were clams, lobsters and other seafood in abundance. When the time came, they would gather round Père Rasle and tell him with great formality that the corn was low and that the tribe must have food, imploring him to come with them to the shore so that they should not be deprived of spiritual comfort.

Invariably, Rasle would answer with a single Indian word: *"Kekiberba"* — "I am listening, my children."

Invariably, they would reply in their language, "We thank you!"

Then they would break camp, with Père Rasle carrying the pine board he used as an altar at home, which would now serve as their church.

Rasle disclaimed all warlike intentions. William Carlos Williams tells of a debate between Rasle and the Governor of Massachusetts in a time of truce. The Governor asked Rasle directly whether, if war were to break out, he would send his Indians after the English. Rasle's response, according to his own account in *lettres edifiantes,* was that *"mon réligion et mon charactère de Prètre, ne m'engageoint à ne leur donner que des conseils de paix"* — or "my religion and my position as a priest would not allow me to give them anything but counsels of peace."

Rasle was, nevertheless, a marked man, with a price on his head of a thousand English pounds. And so gradually the ring tightened around him.

York was headquarters for the campaign of 1723-24, and the force that destroyed Norridgewock after several attempts — although under the overall command of Col. Thomas Westbrook of Portsmouth, for whom the city of Westbrook, Maine, is named — was very much a York affair. Three company commanders in the tough Ranger outfit were from York: Johnson Harmon, who had once been captured by Indians, barely escaping with his life; Jeremiah Moulton, now a hardy frontiersman of thirty-three, who kept the memory of his parents' death as well as of his own childhood escape; and Lewis Bane, a member of the Legislature who had his father's slaying to avenge — and whose brother Joseph, formerly a captive of the Indians, now served as a valuable interpreter.

Jeremiah Moulton's surprise attack on Norridgewock came in the dead of winter. Both Rasle and the Indians, perhaps having been somehow forewarned, were luckily

Drawing of the ancestral Barrell family home, "Barrell's Grove." Nathaniel Barrell, son-in-law of the old Tory, Jonathan Sayward, was York's delagate to the Massachusetts convention that ratified the U. S. Constitution. His daughter, "Madam Wood," was America's first female novelist.

absent. Moulton, who magnanimously refrained from burning the Indian dwellings or Rasle's church, discovered there a letter to Rasle from the Governor of Canada exhorting the priest "to push on the Indians with all imaginable zeal against the English." It was a valuable piece of propaganda.

In 1724, the English tried again. The expedition, by a force of 205 men, commanded by Johnson Harmon, and divided into four companies, with seventeen whaleboats and three Mohawk scouts as guides, arrived at Norridgewock about 3:00 p.m. on the 12th of August. The sixty Indians who met them fired several volleys and then, with the English in hot pursuit, retreated to the river. The fighting continued in the water, as the Indians tried to get into their canoes. According to the account published in a Boston newspaper, Father Rasle organized the defense at Norridgewock, continuing to fire from his house until the English broke down his door and the commander's son-in-law, Lt. Richard Jacques, rushed in and shot the Jesuit through the head. In another version, Rasle was slain next to the rude cross he had erected at the center of the village where he stood so as to draw English bullets upon himself, thus enabling the women and children to escape. The statement in several accounts, that Rasle's body was horribly mutilated ("with his bones all crushed within him"), is declared by others to be pure French propaganda. Possibly contributing to the confusion was the fact that Rasle had been a partial cripple since his youth, the victim of an accidental fracturing of both of his thighs, each of which had mended badly.

The attack on Norridgewock left twenty-seven dead, according to news stories. The attackers brought back four captives, a woman and three children. The Boston newspaper account concludes by declaring: "The abovesaid Ralle [sic], the Jesuit, has generally appeared at the Head of the Indians in their Rebellion and was the Chief Fondater of this war."

Amid widespread rejoicing, Johnson Harmon was promoted to Lieutenant Colonel. But because of his killing of Rasle, Lieutenant Jacques received a reprimand from Capt. Jeremiah Moulton, who as his immediate superior had given orders that Rasle was to be taken alive. The intention had been to force Rasle to admit in a show trial the role of the French clergy in spurring the Indians on to fight. Adding to the shock was the fact that Rasle had been scalped along with the Indian dead.

That the man who killed Rasle should have borne a French surname is an unexplained irony. Possibly Lieutenant Jacques was of Huguenot descent. Since the revocation of the Edict of Nantes in 1685, French Protestants had been fleeing their homeland for the English colonies. Among them were a number bearing names that would become nationally prominent, such as Bowdoin, Delano, Jay, Faneuil, and Revere. Lieutenant Jacques himself later moved eastward to what is now Harpswell, Maine, and was killed there by Indians a few years afterward.

For the English, the death of the Reverend Mr. Dummer had been avenged. For the Indians, the Norridgewock raid was simply a blow from which they never recovered. From then on, despite a fifth Indian War, York experienced no more Indian raids.

York Before the Revolution

A picture of what life was like in York during the years before the Revolution has been preserved in a diary for the year 1735. It tells of arrivals and departures, of land bought and sold, of births, deaths, and marriages. Many of the names that recur — Nowell, Donnell, Card, Stover, Webber, Junkins, Moulton, Young — are still common in York. But some things are no longer the same. In an intriguing reference to an outmoded custom concerning amatory matters, it is recorded that "one Caleb Young gave in to the Town Clerk his intentions to marry Julia Reardon, but she forbid the publishment." More serious was an epidemic of diphtheria, known as the "throat distemper," for which in 1735 there was no known remedy other than prayer and Days of Fasting. Many children died. On the birthday of King George II, loyal toasts were drunk to his health although "there was not much spirit owing to the Distemper." There was crime and there was punishment. Since 1718 the court had held its sessions in York, as it would continue to do until 1832. In 1735 an Indian woman, possibly one of the prisoners brought back from Norridgewock, was hanged for murder. Although those found guilty of adultery were no longer branded on the cheek with an *A* — as one York woman had been during the mid-1600's — not only the gallows at Stage Neck, but also a whipping post ("the Puritan Maypole") was still in use.

The chief moral influence in York for almost forty years had been the Reverend Samuel Moody. In January 1735, he preached a memorable sermon concerning a young man who had recently slipped on the ice and died of an internal hemorrhage — but not before repenting his ill-spent life and leaving his money for the purchase of Bibles. All through the dozen years that still remained of his ministry, Parson Moody would continue to hold up the example of this "Sinful Young Man Who Repented On His Death Bed." By persisting in such eloquence, Moody had helped convert York from its wild early ways to something more Puritan, if not yet wholly sedate. He would later be responsible for bringing the flamboyant English evangelist George Whitefield to York, where he occupied the pulpit of Moody's own First Congregational Church on Sunday, November 4, 1744. There were those in York who preferred "the good old time religion," with its droning, intellectual sermons, to the excitement and showmanship of Whitefield's call for "repentant sinners to come forth and be saved." But despite the strong feelings aroused by the controversial evangelist, who was a personal friend of the parson's, his appearance in the town seems to have had little effect on Moody's own standing.

Moody's standing was such, in fact, that the parish he served readily supplied him with things of this world, including slaves (a part of life in York that would continue until after the Revolution; the town's population in 1765 included some fifty-six slaves). The town records show a vote in January, 1733, that "there be a Slave Bought by the Parish to be imployed for the use of said Parish in Labouring for the Rev. Mr. Samuel Moody." A Negro had been duly bought for him, but in 1735 it was voted that "if the Negro Man can't do for Mr. Moody that the Assessors hire a Man for Mr. Moody." It is also recorded that his household in 1736 included a Negro slave girl named Phyllis.

Despite such special perquisites and despite all the moral and social restrictions on freedom of action, the English settlements were accorded far greater freedom than the French, with their "seigneuries" or feudal estates dominated by the centralized authority of an absolutist government and a far more powerful clergy. It has been said, indeed, that the relative formlessness and diversity of the English settlements is what saved them and made independence possible.

War on Canada

As the threat of the Indians had diminished, that of the French appeared more dire. French immigration into Canada was increasing. In 1744, Gov. William Shirley of Massachusetts proposed to strike a devastating blow against the French fortress of Louisbourg on Cape Breton Island. The stronghold at Louisbourg, which guarded the mouth of the St. Lawrence and was a refuge from which privateers could attack and seize the vessels of New England fishermen plying the Grand Banks, had twice been taken by the English and twice handed back, in 1632 and 1713.

Shirley's plan received grudging approval from the Massachusetts General Court. Empowered to raise 3,000 volunteers, he was also instructed to write the governments of New York, New Jersey, Pennsylvania, New Hampshire, Connecticut and Rhode Island for "their respective Quotas of Men and Vessels." Eventually Shirley received commitments from all of the existing New England provinces, with outright rejections from New Jersey and Pennsylvania, while New York contributed only ten cannon. Benjamin Franklin, who was then a member of the Pennsylvania Legislature, wrote of his skepticism to his brother in Boston:

> Fortified towns are hard nuts to crack and your teeth have not been accustomed to it. Taking strong places is a particular trade which you have taken up without serving an apprenticeship to it. Armies and veterans need skillful engineers to direct them in their attack. Have you any? But some seem to think forts are as easy taken as snuff.[6]

---

[6] There is a letter, signed by Benjamin Franklin, at the original Pepperrell homestead in Kittery Point, indicating that some money was sent from Pennsylvania for the Louisbourg expedition.

To command his New England forces, Shirley carefully avoided choosing from among the ambitious politicians who stepped forward to offer their services. Instead, he singled out William Pepperrell (later Sir William), a wealthy merchant of Kittery, Maine, who had been a member of the Massachusetts General Court since 1727 and president of the Council in 1745, and who was also a colonel of the Maine militia. Pepperrell, competent and extremely popular, was the perfect choice — except that he didn't want the assignment. His wife was ailing, and he questioned his own ability to lead the expedition, though he was strongly in favor of it. Before he made up his mind, Pepperrell went for advice to the evangelist, George Whitefield, a close friend. Pepperrell at last consented, after Whitefield told him that:

> . . . if he (Pepperrell) did undertake it, he (Whitefield) would beg of the Lord God of Armies to give him a single eye; that the means proposed to take Louisbourg, in the eye of human reason, were not more adequate to the end, than the sounding of rams' horns to blow down Jericho; but that if Providence really called him, he would return more than conqueror.

The news of Pepperrell's appointment spurred enlistments, nowhere more than in York, where there was great excitement over the news that a neighbor from Kittery was in command. Col. Jeremiah Moulton was assigned to lead the Third Maine Regiment, and Dr. Alexander Bulman of York became General Pepperrell's personal physician. That old Indian fighter Johnson Harmon wrote begging to take part. Of 3,250 Massachusetts men, a third were from York County.

The expedition assumed the aspect of a holy war, a Protestant Crusade. The Reverend Mr. Whitefield gave it his official blessing with a motto that appeared on Pepperrell's banner: *"Nil desperandum Christo duce* (Despair not with Christ as leader)." In a poem, one Protestant divine implored the Almighty:

> Destroy proud Anti-Christ, O Lord
> And quite consume the Whore.

As chaplain of the Maine troops, the venerable Samuel Moody sailed with the men on a Sunday, preaching from the text "Thy people shall be willing in the day of thy power."

Indeed, the phenomenon of so much prayer drew critical comment from the still skeptical Benjamin Franklin, who wrote again to his brother:

> You have a fast and prayer for that purpose [the fall of Louisbourg]; in which I compute five hundred thousand petitions were offered up to the same effect in New England, which added to the petition of every family morning and evening, multiplied by the number of days since January 25th make forty-five millions of prayers; which, set against the prayers of a few priests in the Garrison to the Virgin Mary, give a vast balance in your favor . . . in attacking strong towns, I should have more dependence on *works,* than on *faith* . . .

Yet Franklin was proved wrong in his misgivings. Aided by a Royal Naval squadron under Commodore Peter Warren and a Colonial squadron under Commodore Edward Tyng of Falmouth, Maine, (now Portland), the New England army successfully laid siege to the French fortress. It fell within six weeks.

Pepperrell and Tyng were instant heroes. Bells rang and cannon roared for an event that impressed itself indelibly on the Colonial mind. It was an *American* victory, accomplished almost entirely without British help. But it had cost the Colonial governments close to £ 200,000 — and all for nought!

Three years later, under the Treaty of Aix-la-Chappelle, the British, for reasons of policy, returned Louisbourg to the French a third time.

It was such politically stupid actions that outraged the people of New England against the British government. Although the climax was still almost thirty years away, Louisbourg was another milestone on the way to the Revolution.

The culmination of the Anglo-Gallic struggle for supremacy came with Wolf's victory over Montcalm at Quebec, where a York native, Col. Jedediah Preble, led a provincial regiment in which there were thirty soldiers from York.

One episode in this era that deserves mention in connection with York, was the banishment to Louisiana of the French inhabitants of Nova Scotia. Thanks to Longfellow's "Evangeline," the plight of these "Acadians" lives on as a shameful memory for the English-speaking world. In fact, many of the exiles did not go to Louisiana but settled in Maine (especially the St. John Valley of northern Aroostook County) and elsewhere throughout the English colonies. It is estimated that in 1760 there were over a thousand Acadians in the Province of Massachusetts. And it is on record that in 1761 twenty-one Acadians were living in York as paupers, having been deprived of their property and goods. The sum of £30 was paid to York by the Province for their maintenance. Although a few of their names are to be found in the town archives — La Vallee-Gillard, Murdeu, Fontaine, Mellin, and most startling, one Stephen Decatur, whose relation to the famed American patriot isn't known — the presence of the Acadians left no lasting mark on the town, but has something of the same sad and misty evanescence as Evangeline's search through the bayous of the Southland for her lost lover. For the record, it should be noted that Stephen Longfellow, the poet's grandfather, taught school in York at a time when there might still have been some Acadians there.

Steps Toward the Revolution

By 1763, York had a degree of security. The growth of other towns, notably Wells to the east and Berwick to the north, left York less exposed, and for the first time since the century began, no quota of men from York was called up for duty elsewhere in guarding the Province. But the time was not far off when men would be called up once more. For the passage of the Stamp Act by Parliament on January 10, 1765, may be considered the beginning of the Revolution no less than the first musket ball loosed at Lexington ten years later. Fired by resentment, Colonial mobs dealt in their own way with the customs officials enforcing the hated law. Tarring and feathering was not uncommon. When, in March, 1776, this bitterly unfair measure was repealed, the colonists rejoiced. But their joy was short-lived as Parliament returned an even more onerous list of duties, on such items as paper, glass, painters' colors, and tea.

In Massachusetts, the General Court met to deal with

The mouth of the York River and the "lower town," or what is now known as York Harbor.

the latest crisis. A resolution to invite the twelve other colonies to form a Confederation in order to deal with the British was offered and passed overwhelmingly despite the opposition of the royalist governor, Francis Bernard, among whose hostile acts was his habitual denial of charters to new towns in Maine, for fear that their representatives to the General Court might be unfavorable to the king. Meanwhile, the town of York was represented by a die-hard Tory sympathizer, Jonathan Sayward, who spoke as well as voted against the patriotic resolution.

Son of the deacon Joseph Sayward, whose debts the town had paid in 1735, Sayward had described himself successively as a "laborer," a "coaster," and a "trader." Like many another merchant, shipowner and self-made man, with his rapid rise to fortune he became a political conservative. His friendship with British authorities cleared the way for a series of appointments — as Justice of the Peace, Justice of the Quorum, Special Justice of the Court of Common Pleas, and Judge of Probate for York County. Judicial posts were then held "at the pleasure of the King," a bone of contention with Colonial assemblies who wanted the power to remove judges. Sayward's election to public office followed in 1766. In the election of 1768, which saw 129 votes cast — the largest total in York's history to date — Sayward received 67, Captain Grow 40, and Captain Bragdon 22.

But 1768 was also the year of what was called the Rescinding Controversy. The British government, finding the Massachusetts resolution "highly inflammatory and tending to sedition," ordered the General Court to rescind it. A vote was taken with seventeen for rescinding and ninety-two opposed. The "Anti-Rescinders" were immediately lionized in verse and song, in the columns of newspapers, and in innumerable toasts at banquets, while the seventeen "Rescinders" earned notoriety, scorn, and hatred to an equal degree. Paul Revere made a silver punch bowl dedicated to the "Immortal 92," and also drew a caricature that showed the seventeen being driven into hell. This was a favorite theme. A contemporary poem begins:

On brave Rescinders to yon yawning cell
Seventeen such miscreants will sure startle Hell.

Representative Sayward, needless to say, was among the seventeen Rescinders. That he was out of step with his constituents was soon evident. At a town meeting on September 13, 1768, York voted that "this Town highly approve of the Proceedings of those of the late Hon. House of Representatives who were not for rescinding . . . that this Town sincerely thank the late Hon. House of Representatives, who were for maintaining our Just Rights and Liberties."

John Adams, who would one day be president of the United States, as a lawyer was a frequent visitor to pre-Revolutionary York for sessions of the Court. In the thick of activities that led to the Revolution, he took care to be informed on the sympathies of persons of influence in a community. Not long after the Rescinding controversy, he wrote:

> David Sewall is not of the liberty side; the Moultons, Lymans and Sewalls and Saywards are all of the prerogative side. They are afraid of their commissions; and rather than hazard them they would ruin the country. We had a fair trial of them when we met to return thanks to the ninety-two anti-rescinders; none of them voted for it though none of them but Sayward and his bookkeeper had courage enough to hold up his hand when the vote was put the contrary way.

This fair-minded if grudging respect for Judge Sayward's courage was of a piece with Adams' own defense in court, as a matter of principle, of the British officer in charge at the Boston massacre. On the other hand, Adams' harsh judgment of others at York was not entirely borne out by later events. Judge David Sewall, for example, later became a staunch supporter of the "liberty side."

Adams also left a vivid description for posterity of what it was like to be welcomed to York for a session of the Court: "When I got to the tavern on the eastern side of the Piscataqua River, I found the Sheriff of York [Jotham Moulton] and six of his deputies, all with gold laced hats, ruffles, swords and very gay clothes, all likely young men, who had come to that place ten miles, to escort the Court into town . . ."

It was at a dinner meeting during one of these visits

that Adams and Sayward, in a spirited exchange, recalled the part played by the Reverend Samuel Moody in the Louisbourg expedition:

> *Sayward:* Mr. Adams, you are going to the [Continental Congress] and great things are in agitation. I recommend to you the doctrine of my former minister, Mr. Moody. Upon an occasion of some gloomy prospects for the country, he preached a sermon from this text — "They know not what they do." After a customary introduction, he raised this doctrine from his text, that in times of great difficulty and danger, when men know not what to do, it is the duty of a person or a people to be very careful that they do not do they know not what.
>
> *Adams:* But I thought the venerable preacher, when he had beat the drum ecclesiastic to animate the country to undertake the expedition to Louisbourg in 1745 and had gone with it himself as a chaplain, had ventured to do he knew not what, as much as I am likely to do in the expedition to Congress. I must trust Providence as Mr. Moody had done when he did his duty, though he could not foresee the consequences.

In 1772, the town of York expressed itself through a resolution calling for "speedy redress of . . . grievances so burthensome and distressing to us . . ." In 1774, the report of a distinguished committee of townspeople who had been directed to express the town's sentiments on the continuing crisis contained a number of familiar-sounding assertions, such as:

> That the People in the British American Colonies, by their Constitution of Government, have a Right to Freedom and an Exemption from every Degree of Oppression and Slavery.
>
> That it is an essential Right of Freemen to have the Disposal of their own Property and not be Tax'd by any Power over which they can have no control.
>
> That the Parliamentary Duty Laid upon Teas Landed in America for the Express purpose of raising a Revenue, is in effect a Tax upon the Americans, without their consent.

From this it can be inferred that the most tangible grievance was the detested duty upon tea. Patriotic American housewives were boycotting the beverage. Since the occasion known as the Boston Tea Party was the strongest of the protests, the first act of retribution by the British was aimed at Massachusetts. The port of Boston was closed. Parliament altered the Massachusetts Charter, increasing the arbitrary powers of the Governor, changing the manner of choosing jurors and providing that those accused of certain crimes were to be tried in England.

Jonathan Sayward's own feelings about the Boston Tea Party were expressed in a diary entry for December 17, 1773: "The men of Belial arose in boston and took Possession of the 2 ships of tea and hoisted them all out and turned it into the Dock."

At a two-day town meeting on whether or not to approve the Boston Tea Party, he argued in vain for the royalist position — that the duty upon tea was neither a tax nor an imposition since it left up to the people whether to use tea or not and further that the dumping of tea was malicious destruction of property. Still not without influence, he was able to have the resolution softened — but not to prevent York from holding its own "Tea Party."

There can be little doubt that York was used as a port to evade British duties. What is known as the John Hancock Warehouse, off Lindsay Road along the York River (now restored, it is on the National Register of Historic Places) is said to have been taken over by John Hancock, through the foreclosure of a mortgage, as yet another hideaway for goods smuggled past the customs inspectors. It is known that Hancock was arrested at least once for evading the tax on Madeira wine, and that his ship was confiscated. But circumstances made Hancock a patriot rather than a mere bootlegger. It is probable that his warehouse in York would have held mostly rum and tea.

But what happened to a non-patriot who brought in tea is another story — and that is what happened at the "York Tea Party." In it, once again, we find Jonathan Sayward going against the grain of the majority. On September 15, 1774, the sloop *Cynthia,* commanded by Sayward's nephew Capt. James Donnell, arrived from Newfoundland with a cargo of 150 pounds of tea. When word circulated that there was tea in the harbor, a committee was chosen to seize the merchandise. This was done openly, through a town meeting. The goods were taken openly and deposited "for safe keeping" in the store of Capt. Edward Grow near Sewall's Bridge. On the following night, however, a party of "Pickwacket Indians" broke into the store and carried off the tea, which was never seen again. That, at least, is one version of the story. As Jonathan Sayward recorded it in his diary, the tea was anonymously replaced two days later. The incident increased the bad feeling against him, and there were unfounded rumors that he would be attacked by a mob.

During that same month of September, 1774, the Continental Congress passed a Declaration of Rights. A town meeting held at York the following January approved all of its fourteen articles, and elected Capt. Daniel Bragdon to represent the town in a Massachusetts Congress the next month. Among his instructions was the admonition "That to your utmost, you endeavour to prevent every Measure that shall lead the Province into a Civil War."

But Bragdon also received the contrary instructions "That you do nothing that shall Militate with the proceedings of the late Continental Congress, and that you do not consent or advise to any Infraction upon the Laws of the Province of the Massachusetts Bay made and enacted under the Royal Charter of William and Mary."

At this late date accommodation was next to impossible. Only weeks remained before the climactic date of April 19, 1775, when the shooting began at Lexington and Concord.

The Revolution

With American guns fired against the authority of the British Crown, rebellion was in the open. What was more, the regular soldiers of the British Army, the feared and hated "redcoats" or "lobsterbacks," had taken a pounding from the farmers of eastern Massachusetts. Their retreat to Boston, although professionally conducted, was very much in the nature of a rout.

The dramatic events at Concord and Lexington aroused enthusiasm everywhere in the colonies. Spontaneously, patriotic groups armed. In some instances, these irregular bodies went directly after British forces. To the small

Down East settlement of Machias, Maine, goes the honor of being the site of the first naval battle of the Revolution. It was here, on June 12, 1775, that the inhabitants of a primitive lumbering community attacked and then captured the British naval vessel *Margaretta*. In hand-to-hand fighting many of the forty Americans were armed solely with pitchforks, and at least two of them were killed. But so were ten of the English, including their commander, Captain Moor, who had sparked the action when he ordered the Machiasites to take down a liberty pole celebrating the news of Lexington and Concord.

Another precipitate action by colonists in Maine, the seizure of several British naval officers in May 1775, led to the shelling and burning five months later of Falmouth (now Portland) by the British. The direct causal relationship was a Captain Mowatt, one of the May captives, who, eventually released, returned in October with a squadron to bombard the city. Among the 130 buildings destroyed was an Anglican Church, St. Paul's. Miraculously, not a single person was killed.

Maine saw no major Revolutionary battles. Aside from the two incidents just described, an ill-fated expedition to the Loyalist stronghold of Bagaduce (now Castine), and Arnold's disastrous march to Quebec were the only military engagements to shatter the relative peace. There was a considerable amount of privateering off the coast, and the strong groups of Loyalists who congregated near the mouth of the Penobscot River under the protection of British occupation forces also constituted a threat.

A little remembered aspect of the war was an abortive attempt by the British government to create a new province out of territory covering much of what is now Maine. It was to extend from the Saco to the St. Croix River, and was to be called "New Ireland." The document in which the proposal was made is instructive as an example of the autocratic English mentality. "It has been found by sad experience," reads one revealing sentence, "that the Democratic power is predominant in all parts of British America." Still more revealing is the statement that New Ireland was to be organized

> To reward or Indemnify the Loyal Sufferers from the other Provinces, and at the same time lay the ground

for an Aristocratic Power, the Lands to be granted in large Tracts to the most Meritorious and to be by them leased to the lower People in manner as has been practiced in New York, which is the only Province in which there is a Tenantry, and was the least inclined to Rebellion. The poorest Loyal Sufferers should however have Grants from the Crown.

The province of New Ireland died before it could be born.

In York itself, as elsewhere, the news of Concord and Lexington galvanized men into action. At 9:00 p.m. on the day of the battle, a post rider arrived to tell of the momentous fight. The next morning, the village green was alive with people as a militia company was constituted.

Records of such a company at York go back as far as 1654. A continuing institution after the outbreak of the first Indian War in 1676, the militia or "train band" spawned the custom of "muster days," which were more like boisterous holidays than training exercises. Somewhere along the way — with the quantities of spirits consumed — there arose the tradition of a "muster day gingerbread" which was served to the crowds who gathered for the occasion.

But in York on the morning of April 21, 1775, all was business. The men came with long-barreled flintlocks, probably of many different designs and origins. Likewise there was little uniformity in their dress, although a few may have had uniforms or pieces of uniforms from the French and Indian Wars. Capt. Johnson Moulton, a relative of old Johnson Harmon and also a veteran of several campaigns against the French, was put in command, and the men of York marched off toward Massachusetts and their embattled brethren. Sixty-one strong, they were financed by a special grant of £200 from the county treasurer, and included one Cesar, a slave.

According to all accounts, the York militia marched to Portsmouth, crossed the Piscataqua by ferry, and moved southward another fifteen miles before they bivouacked for the night. There is no evidence that they moved on; most probably having learned that their services were not needed, they returned to York. In May they were reor-

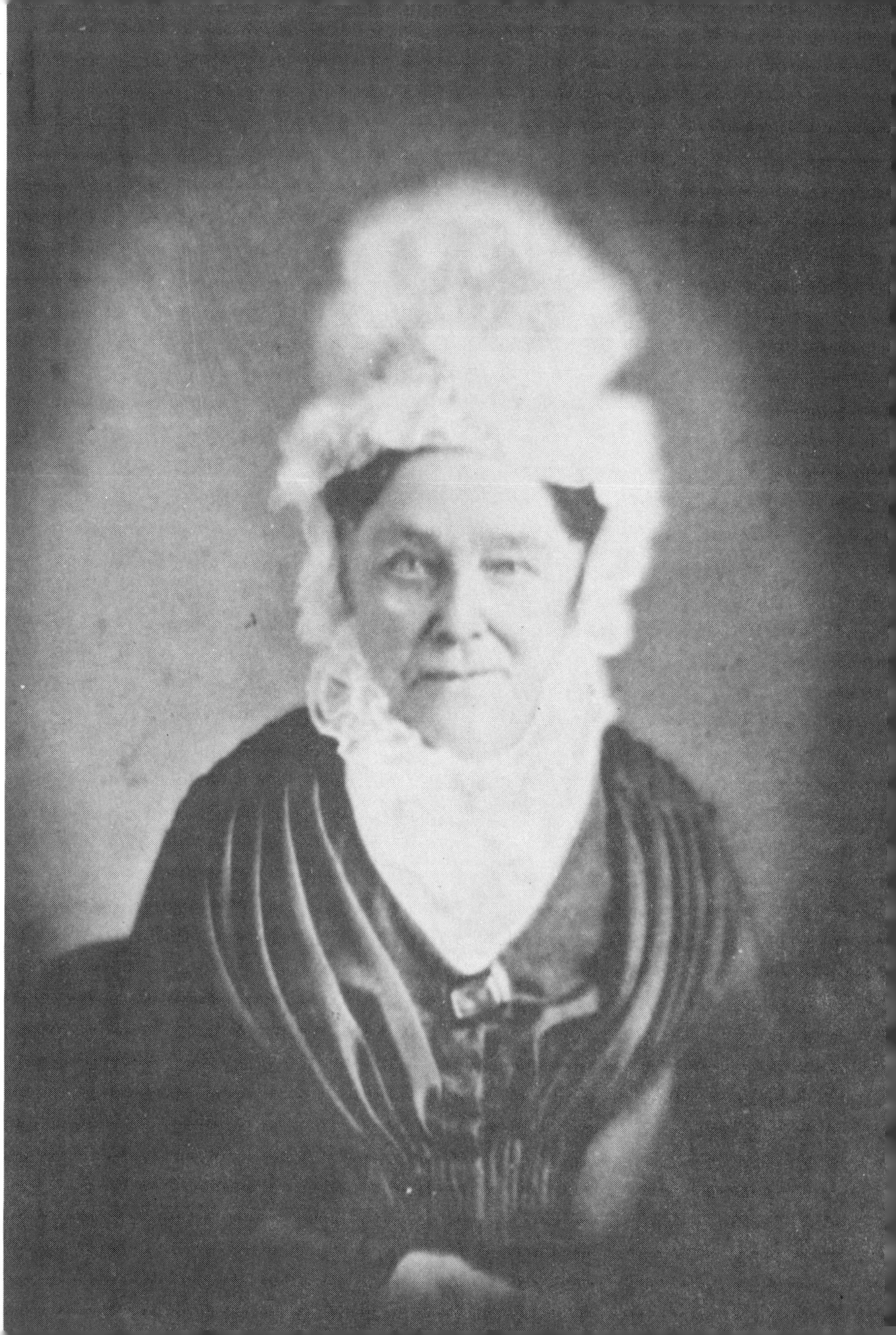

ganized under the command of Maj. Samuel Derby, who had emigrated to York eight years earlier.[7]

On the home front, special town meetings were held to raise money to establish a military night watch for the harbor, to procure emergency corn, and to form Committees of Correspondence and Inspection. The latter, after a close interrogation of Jonathan Sayward, concluded that he was harmless. On June 5, 1776, forewarned that Congress might declare independence, a York town meeting formally advised its Representative, Joseph Simpson, almost a full month in advance, that the town had voted, "that if the Honorable Congress should for the safety of the Colonies declare them independent of the Kingdom of Great Britain that the said inhabitants will solemnly engage with their lives and fortunes to support them in the measure."

In the struggle that continued until the defeat of Cornwallis at another town of York (Yorktown, Virginia), soldiers from its namesake in Maine saw service in many battles. During the terrible winter of 1777 and 1778, Samuel Derby was at Valley Forge along with more than a dozen volunteers from York. Lt. Moses Banks, of York, served on George Washington's staff. Other York men fought at Ticonderoga, Monmouth, Saratoga, and Castine.

York seamen were likewise active, many as privateers, some as members of the fledgling American navy. Several served with John Paul Jones; in fact, the second in command on his ship, *Ranger,* built in nearby Portsmouth, N.H., was a York man, Thomas Simpson. After a brief but distinguished maiden career — she was the first American ship to fly the American flag, the first to receive a salute from a foreign nation (France), the first to engage in hit-and-run raids on the English coast, the first to score a victory over a British man-of-war — the *Ranger* sailed back to America under Simpson's command. Jones had given the order with twin motives — he couldn't stand

Madam Wood–
Sally Sayward Barrell
(c. 1800).

---

[7] He had held (and would resume after the war) the official title of Culler of Hoops and Staves, one of several positions — such as Sealers of Leather, Corders of Wood, and Surveyors of Lumber — that trace to the ancient craft guilds of England and whose function was to guarantee the quality of their respective materials to the customer.

Simpson, and he had now secured a ship that was more to his liking, *Le Bonhomme Richard*.[8]

But privateering was the venture that most notably affected York. Four men from the town who served on the privateer *Dalton,* which was captured by the British in 1776, wound up in England's Dartmoor Prison. And Jonathan Sayward's diary is full of entries such as these:

> August 4, 1780: Captain Grow in a Privateer Returned from a Cruise and brought in to York a ten gun Privateer and a schooner loaded for the W. Indies.
>
> July 4, 1781: a number of Kings vessels of war and Privateers in our Bay taking great many coasters and prisoners.
>
> August 20, 1781: Raynes in his schooner fitted as a Privateer returned this day with a Prize ship of 200 tons burden, Cargo 2,000 bushels of salt, 37 hogsheads sugar, etc.

A puzzling entry came after Cornwallis's defeat at Yorktown in October 1781. On March 13, 1782, Sayward wrote: "hear 5 sail of our vessels taken by Brig Privateer from Bagaduce [Castine]." It was not until April 29, 1783, that he set down the much-quoted "a day of Public Rejoicing on hearing of peace . . . Carried to excess in breaking the wheels and gun carriages all to pieces. Suppose we should never want them any more."

Notwithstanding his use of "our" and "we," as though he had always sided with the rebellious colonists, Sayward must have viewed the American victory with mixed feelings. Since according to his beliefs, it couldn't have happened, his support for England was no more than might be expected of any sane and reasonable man. Sayward is an interesting example of the Tory sympathizer who never betrayed his own countrymen. The outbreak of the Revolution found him publicly forced to explain his correspondence with British officials. During the war, he lived virtually as a prisoner. His wife died on September 12, 1775. His diary contains a list of his woes:

---

[8] The French translation of the "Poor Richard" of Benjamin Franklin's famous almanac; by thus naming the warship, France honored Franklin, who was immensely popular as America's Special Envoy.

> I have lost a new Sloop Cast away this month and Suffered the Loss of one or more Cargoes in West Indies . . . I have been Confined upon my honor not to absent my Self from the town . . . often threatened . . . all my offices as Judge of Probate, Judge of Court of Common Pleas, Justice of Quorum, Justice of Peace taken from me . . . Constant Danger of being Driven from my Habitation so much that I have constantly kept $200 Lawfull in Gold and paper currency in my Pocket . . . I have been examined before Committees and obliged to Lay open my Letters from Governor Hutchinson . . .

The Declaration of Independence astounded him. "It's all Beyond my Depth," he wrote. "I am lost in Wonder."

Because Sayward's Toryism took the form of a benign loyalty to England rather than a fiery hatred of the colonists' cause, he was really treated rather well. Most Tories were handled far less gently. Atrocity tales of what happened to them are legion. Most were uprooted from their homes or exiled themselves voluntarily. Nova Scotia and the Bahamas received large contingents. With the advent of peace, many of those suspected of "Toryism" were persecuted, imprisoned, and summarily deprived of their property.

Jonathan Sayward was lucky. Although he lost his offices, suffered financially, and endured personal indignities, for the most part the people of York left him alone. Obviously, they remembered his past services as a comrade in arms from the attack on Louisbourg. There was always a certain respect for his character and his courage. Eventually, with the war over, he even regained some of his former social position. He entertained the judges of the court at his home. Like his father, he became an elder of the church. In 1785, he was host in York to a visiting Italian nobleman, Count Luigi Castiglioni, then a young man of twenty-three who had arrived from Milan for a tour of the United States.

Six years later, the old judge received a truly illustrious visitor — John Hancock, governor of Massachusetts. The two had been friends before the Revolution. The governor's grandfather, the Reverend John Hancock, had preached in York for two years, from 1694 to 1696, as the immediate successor to the martyred Reverend Dummer. The judge set down this mellow entry in his diary: "Governor Hancock and Lady and his Sute paid me an agreeable visit and dined with a large company with which he honoured me and in confidence regained my judgment of men for the good of the country in which I hope I have done some service."

Sayward died on May 8, 1797, the richest man in York. A newspaper obituary reported as though by way of epitaph: "A very large and respectable collection of citizens on the 11th. ultimo, with undissembled marks of esteem, respect and affection, attended the interment of this amiable, good man."

A New Nation

Severed from England, the thirteen Atlantic Seaboard colonies had to cope with the task of governing themselves. So far as the Province of Massachusetts was concerned, the effort had begun long before the outcome of the war could be certain. As early as June 1777, a committee was at work on a Massachusetts Constitution, which was submitted to town meetings less than a year later. York took action on May 11, 1778, with a record number of 147 ballots cast. They were unanimously against approval of the document.

At another vote in 1779, York was still unanimously opposed. Then, at a convention of Massachusetts towns, with David Sewall representing York, a revised draft was offered. York referred it to a special committee, which suggested that it be adopted, but with amendments: "That the Governor and Council, more especially the Governor, shall be of the Protestant Religion: That Military Officers be appointed by the Governt. with the advice and consent of the Council: That the Power Suspending the Habeus Corpus be confined to Six Months: That the Revisal and Amendment (if need be) of the Constitution instead of 15 years shall be done in Ten . . ."

Judge Sewall was asked, as Representative, to do his best to secure the amendments. He failed, but the Constitution passed. York lived under it for forty years.

David Sewall was becoming not only a leading citizen of York, but also one of its most distinguished ever. His support for the Massachusetts Constitution may well have persuaded his contemporaries to accept it. As a member of the General Court, he served on the committee of seven who drafted the document. In many respects, his career as Justice of the Quorum, Justice of the Superior Court, Justice of the Peace, and Register of Probate, paralleled that of his friend, Jonathan Sayward. Politically, however, Sewall differed with him in giving full support to independence. He was chairman of the York Committee of Correspondence, organized after the battles of Concord and Lexington.

Sewall's crowning distinction was to be named by President George Washington as the first federal judge in Maine, where he presided over the United States District Court for twenty-eight years. Altogether, he was more than forty-one years on the bench. During the first presidential election, in 1788, he was Maine's only presidential elector. He was a charter member of the American Academy of Arts and Sciences, and an organizer of the Massachusetts Historical Society. His interest in education led him to the presidency of the Board of Overseers of Bowdoin College. The splendid mansion he built in York — called Conventry Hall after the Sewall's ancestral home in England — is still standing.

A different person entirely was Nathaniel Barrell, who figured in the ratification of the United States Constitution. In the outcome of the fiery debate over the document, which had to be ratified by nine of the thirteen states before it went into effect, Massachusetts was pivotal. The unworkability of the Articles of Confederation had become obvious. No firm national authority existed to deal effectively with national problems. Pockets of disorder had already appeared. Shays's Rebellion in Massachusetts, led by a former officer in Washington's army and mainly expressing a desire for easier money and relief from creditors, spread fear among the more conservative and established groups in society. The answer to such fears was the United States Constitution — a document unique in history and one that has lent stability to American institutions for almost two hundred years.

But at the time, the feelings against the proposed Constitution were as strong as those in favor. And in York the most vocal opponent was Nathaniel Barrell.

As Jonathan Sayward's son-in-law, Barrell was reputed to have been a Tory himself. In the decade preceding the Revolution, he had joined a religious sect known as "Glassites" or "Sandemanians" after its founders, which held to the theological tenet of "rendering unto Caesar the things that are Caesar's," and thus supported the position that King George had the right to levy taxes. Barrell came to live in York after being more or less driven out of Portsmouth, N.H. Although he never got along well with Jonathan Sayward, he was likewise kept under surveillance during the war and was not allowed to participate in military affairs.

It is clear that sentiment in York was strongly against ratifying the proposed Constitution, for both of the delegates chosen at a town meeting in 1787 to represent its citizens at the Boston convention were outspoken opponents. The York townspeople made their sentiments still clearer by naming Barrell, despite his Tory antecedents and despite his behaving so intemperately at the meeting that he drew a "severe Reprimand from Judge Sewall." Capt. Elias Preble was elected to be his companion. They went to Boston with a clear understanding that they were to stand adamantly against ratification.

The Boston convention dragged on throughout January 1788. Delaware and Pennsylvania had already ratified. Momentum could be won or lost depending on what happened in the Bay State. Alarmed Federalists met with those influential Massachusetts citizens who had reservations, such as Gov. John Hancock and Samuel Adams. A primary objection of many opponents was that such rights as freedom of speech and freedom of the press were not guaranteed by the original draft. Under the compromise that was reached, these guarantees were incorporated as the first ten amendments, known ever since as The Bill of Rights.

There was a dramatic meeting on January 31, 1788, at which Gov. John Hancock, who had been ill, was "borne up the broad aisle in men's arms, his gouty limbs wrapped up in flannels to protect him from the cold," to propose the amendments that were to become the Bill of Rights and then to give an impassioned plea for the Constitution. Samuel Adams next rose to endorse what Hancock had said. In the debate that followed, Nathaniel Barrell also spoke. He expressed many objections, but from the language he used, it was clear that his opposition was softening. His brother had been working to influence him; so had George Thacher of Biddeford, who represented the Maine District in the Continental Congress. Judge David

Sewall later credited Thacher, who was also a good friend of Jonathan Sayward's, with having swayed Barrell. When the vote was taken in Boston, the Constitution was approved by a bare majority of nineteen votes out of 365. Barrell was among those who voted *for* approval.

How he explained his change of heart to those who had sent him to Boston is not specifically recorded. He suffered no public retaliation. And in any event, he wouldn't have cared, as he wrote Congressman Thacher: "I can assure you I place as first among the most meritorious acts of my life my assent to the federal Constitution, notwithstanding I see serious consequences attending on it and that by thus doing I create in this town (at least) temporary enemies of those I considered two months since as disinterested friends."

The action of Massachusetts helped break the logjam, being followed by the ratifications of Maryland, South Carolina, and New Hampshire. By 1789, the Constitution was the law of the land. Ironically, Massachusetts never did get around to ratifying the Bill of Rights, at least not until its 150th Anniversary in 1941 when someone discovered this omission.

Under the new Constitution, George Washington became the nation's first president. The United States could now take its place among the nations of the world.

A New State

The Revolutionary War left the new nation with the burden of a $70-million debt, whose equivalent today would of course be many millions more. Massachusetts — since it had furnished more men for the war than even Virginia, then the wealthiest and most populous state — owed the highest amount, some $5 million. Its towns were required to pay bounties for enlistments. In 1783, York protested to the Massachusetts authorities against a fine of £ 20 per man for having failed to meet enlistment quotas. "In your memorialists' opinion," the Selectmen wrote, "all the money in the Town will not be adequate to discharge one Quarter part of the Continental Taxes already ordered for 1782."

It was partly in response to these assessments that the movement in Maine for independent statehood began. The first public suggestion appears to have been a verse

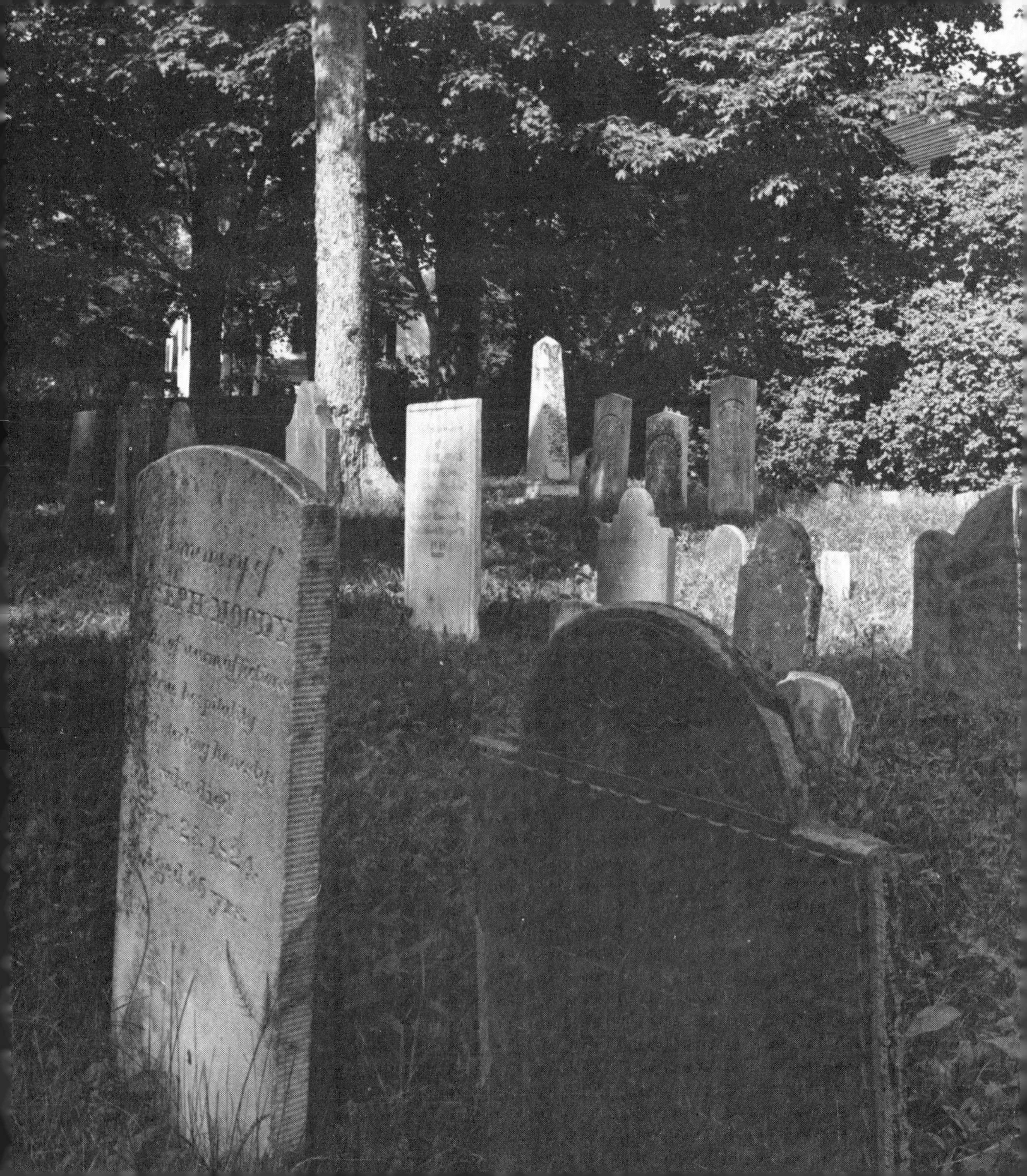

acrostic printed in the Falmouth *Gazette* in 1785, signed with the pseudonym, in the manner of the time, of "a benevolent Gentleman in a neighboring Town." Further articles approving the idea were signed with *noms de plume* — "Ruricola," "Philanthropos," and "Philadelphos," or such veiled designations as "A Farmer" and "A Well-Wisher to the Eastern Country." Thus commenced a movement that was to agitate Maine until statehood was granted in 1820, some thirty-five years later.

Of the leaders of the movement, two had York connections, although the town itself, like most of those along the coast, was at first strongly opposed. The prime mover toward separation was William King, who would later serve as the first governor of Maine. He and his half-brother, Rufus King, later a U.S. Senator from New York, were the sons of Richard King of Scarborough, and grandsons of a York Bragdon. Both men married Bragdon cousins from York. Among the strongest opponents of separation was Stephen Longfellow, father of the poet, whose own father had married into the same Bragdon family. Another major advocate of separation was a future diplomat, William Pitt Preble of Saco, with direct ties to the Preble family of York.

The issue had distinct political overtones. Those against separation were generally adherents of the Federalist party of Washington and John Adams, which was dominant in New England. Statehood supporters were mostly Democrat-Republicans of the party founded by Thomas Jefferson. A referendum was held in 1792. Throughout Maine the vote was close — 2,074 for separation, 2,525 against — but York went overwhelmingly against statehood, 140-1. The identity of the lone supporter was never revealed. By 1797, the votes in favor had risen to three, and the opposition had dwindled to seventy-nine. Statewide, the measure lost once again that year, and yet again in 1807 when York once more voted No.

Then followed the War of 1812.

In New England, this was an extremely unpopular war. The region's thriving international trade came to a virtual standstill except for what was carried on illicitly with the British, much of it through the Maine town of Eastport. During the War of 1812, the British occupied the Maine coast eastward from the Penobscot River. That the Federal government was unable or unwilling to drive the

The old graveyard in York.

British from Yankee soil further added to the antiwar attitude in the Northeast.

Conditions such as these led to the Hartford Convention which was famous, or infamous, as amounting to a secessionist movement. In fact, the convention was little more than a forum to air New England's grievances, contenting itself for the most part with issuing recommendations for a change in the federal system, notably the procedure allowing Southern states to count three-fourths of their slave populations in determining Congressional representation.

But from the point of view of the Federalists, the Hartford Convention was a political disaster, since they were blamed for instigating a treasonous act of disunity while the country was at war. The anti-Federalist opprobrium singled out Stephen Longfellow, who was a delegate from Maine to the Hartford Convention, and noted as a strong opponent of statehood. Sentiment against the Federalists now contributed to a revival of the Maine separation movement. So did a widespread feeling that Massachusetts had let the Down-Easters down by not helping to clear British forces from their territory.

Perhaps typical were the views of a Bangor resident who wrote to William King: "If Massachusetts won't cooperate and the Federal government is unable to, then the crisis has arrived when the District of Maine ought to legislate for herself" — or the declaration of a Democrat-Republican caucus in Oxford County that it was "inexpedient that the District of Maine constitute a part of the state of Massachusetts — no longer than the state of Massachusetts gives support to the union." The Democrat-Republicans, naturally, were quick to seize on a popular political issue to counteract the previous unpopularity of Democrat-Republican Presidents Jefferson and Madison because of their ban on shipping followed by a detested war.

In York, trade had gradually dwindled under the pressures of Jefferson's Embargo and then of the British blockade. A story — probably at least partly apocryphal — is told of an attack in local waters by a British warship, the *Endymion,* on an American sailboat, the *Juno,* and the landing of a British party at York. According to one version of the story, the British were met with musket fire in the vicinity of the Nubble, a promontory where a lighthouse has stood since 1879. Benjamin Donnell of York was said to have shot a British seaman in the same affray — although the log of the *Endymion* does not mention such an incident.

With the end of the war, statehood again became the principal interest in Maine. Massachusetts allowed a new referendum, for which some detected a political motivation — a wish by the Federalists of Massachusetts to separate themselves from a district that was predominantly Democrat-Republican. A crucial vote in September, 1816, gave the separationists a victory — 11,927 to 10,539 — which, however, fell short of the five-ninths majority stipulated by the Massachusetts General Court as necessary. York this time favored separation 126-38. A vote in 1818 finally settled the question, with 17,091 for separation and 7,132 against. York voted for separation, but only by a narrow margin of 151 Yea to 136 Nay.

The suspense was not yet over. There was still the problem of admission to the Union. According to the terms of separation, if Maine had not been admitted as a state by March 4, 1820, the district would revert to Massachusetts. What Congress — or at least its Southern members — intended was to balance the admission of Maine as a Free State with that of Missouri as a Slave State, since there were objections to admitting any further Slave States. Any accommodation, in other words, involved a race against time.

Among the leaders of the anti-slavery forces were Sen. Rufus King and his half-brother William King; their efforts secured a two-year extension of the deadline for Maine's admission to relieve pressure on the Free Staters. Eventually under the Missouri Compromise, both states were admitted, and slavery was prohibited north of 36°30' in all territory of the Louisiana Purchase. On March 15, 1820, Maine was admitted as the twenty-third state of the Union, the tenth to be joined with the original thirteen colonies.

Following Statehood

America was expanding westward. The War of 1812 had witnessed the last fighting on New England territory. Now the influence of the Northeast became proportionately less. The Maine frontier was merely a frontier with

British Canada, and one that became totally peaceable after the conclusion in 1842 of the so-called "Aroostook War," with the Webster-Ashburton Treaty setting the final boundaries between Maine and Canada.

York's history now becomes increasingly parochial, entering into larger national currents only to the degree that the town was part of the nation and that any Americans would be concerned with broader public affairs. Thus, forty years after the Missouri Compromise, which from the beginning contained the seeds of civil war, three-quarters of the men in York were to join the blue-clad armies that would crush Secession. Throughout the intervening years, citizens of York were aware of the controversies raging in the country — Abolitionism, the Dred Scott case, the Fugitive Slave Law, the Kansas disorders, John Brown's raid, and so on.

Impoverished by the decline in shipping after the War of 1812, York found itself hard pressed to meet expenses. The offices of selectmen and tax collector were auctioned off to the *lowest* bidder, in the hope that money could thus be saved on salaries. In 1821 a town meeting article began: "To take fully into consideration the embarrassed state of the financial concerns of the town of York . . ."

There had been periodic attempts to shift the county seat from York. In 1812, some previous objections had been answered by the construction of a new courthouse (today the York Town Hall); nevertheless, these attempts continued. First, the offices of the county treasurer and county clerk went to Kennebunk. Next, Alfred was established as co-county seat along with York, and a fireproof vault for records was built there rather than at York. In 1832, Alfred was irrevocably chosen the county seat. York, more than ever, was now just another Maine town.

Opportunities for employment were limited, despite the opening of the Federal Navy Yard in Kittery after 1800. Young people were leaving. Many moved west, a number of them to the virgin lands of the Western Reserve, in what is now Ohio. A gravestone in York shows how at least one family scattered. Of the four sons of Jonathan S. Keating and Mary Barrell, between 1839 and 1862, one died in New Orleans, one in Washington, D.C., one on a vessel sailing between San Francisco and New York, and one in Salmon Falls, California.

In York itself, efforts to establish industry continued. For more than a century the Chase family operated first a weaving mill and then a woolen factory near Chase's Pond. The factory burned in the late 1870's and was never rebuilt. The York Cotton Factory Company became the first such mill to be incorporated in the State of Maine. After the War of 1812, the company closed down. Other enterprises came and went — a paint factory, a manufacturer of window sashes and blinds, a manufacturer of ladders, a carriage-maker, shipbuilders, and, most recently, several brickyards. Today York itself has no industry. The largest employer is the nearby Kittery-Portsmouth Navy Yard. Tourism is second as a source of employment for York's citizens.

The Growth of Tourism

The first visit of summer tourists to York is said to have been in 1857, when two brothers, John Goddard of Middleborough, Massachusetts, and Samuel Goddard of Brookline, stayed as paying guests at the home of a Mr. and Mrs. Stephen Grant. Whether, indeed, their visit was absolutely the *first* such instance is a moot point. Soon afterward, at any rate, more families — particularly in what was known as the "Lower Town," and later as York Harbor — were taking in boarders. In October 1865, construction was begun on Lord House for Henry C. Lord of Cincinnati, Ohio, or possibly for his father, Nathan Lord, who was president of Dartmouth College. One story has it that the elder Lord was turned away by the Grants and referred to another family because of his political views. (Mrs. Grant was then entertaining associates of such ardent Abolitionists as John Greenleaf Whittier, William Lloyd Garrison, and Wendell Phillips.) Eventually, the Lords purchased a field adjoining the Long Beach section of York Beach, where Lord House was built. Kittery House, another early "cottage," as these large, many-roomed summer houses were called, was built in October 1867, at the eastern end of Long Beach, or Long Sands. It was owned jointly by ten persons.

From such spacious houses that were not quite hotels, it was but a short step to the building of an actual hotel. The first one, built by Maffit W. Bowden, officially opened on June 26, 1869. It burned four years later.

A tennis game at York Harbor in 1888. The site of this long-vanished court is the fishing wharf where the Donnell family has its commercial dock.

Earlier ventures notwithstanding, the acknowledged impetus for the development of York, and especially of York Harbor, into an important resort area was the building in 1871 of the Marshall House.

As its builder, Nathaniel Grant Marshall holds a place in York's history comparable to that occupied by Edward Rishworth, David Sewall, Jonathan Sayward, and Samuel Moody — all major figures in the passing scene of local events. Marshall's life story is pure Horatio Alger. Born into an impoverished family of English emigrants in 1812, just as York was entering a prolonged period of economic depression, Marshall had the further handicap of a birth defect: he came into the world with only one hand. His father disappeared when he was five years old, his mother died when he was seven; at fifteen, after his grandparents died, he was completely on his own. Nevertheless, he forged an impressive career in business, law, and public affairs. He held many offices, including those of town clerk, county sheriff, state senator, collector of customs, and collector of internal revenue for Maine's First District. But the Marshall House was his crowning achievement. A first-class hotel in a magnificent setting, it soon attracted to York Harbor a wealthy and influential circle from the entire country.

The Marshall House was erected on Stage Neck, where hangings had once taken place. One of the most beautiful spots in Maine, before this development it was a badly rundown area, as was all of "Lower Town." As a writer in the Salem (Massachusetts) *Gazette* in 1869 described it, "Her wharves and storehouses now dropping to decay, her streets laid out with so much care and precision, all spoke of a time when she had seen better and more prosperous days." During the Revolution, the Massachusetts General Court had ordered the fishermen living on the offshore Isles of Shoals to evacuate their homes. To do so, the fishermen dismantled and made rafts of their houses, floated them ashore and set them up again. Twenty-two such families had floated to York and set up their dwellings on Stage Neck. This colony, supported by public welfare, remained the poorest in town. Nathaniel Marshall, in an early effort at urban renewal, had these "shoal houses" removed. Some were taken intact to other locations and are still standing today.

"This (Marshall) House," boasts an advertisement

printed in 1896, "is located at York Harbor, Maine, at its very mouth on an elevated point of land, commanding on Ocean and Inland scenery, unsurpassed on the Atlantic seaboard . . . A Telephone and Telegraph office are located in the house. A Livery Stable in proximity. The bathing facilities are excellent. Lawn Tennis. Grounds. Barber Shop, Billiard and Dance Hall are connected with the house. The house possesses every improvement incident to a first class hotel." The original building was of wood; it burned, and was replaced by one made of brick. This second Marshall House was torn down in 1972, to make room for yet another "first class hotel" — the multimillion-dollar Stage Neck Inn, which opened in July 1973. In keeping with recent trends in the vacation industry, the project involved Stage Neck Associates, a group of long-time York Harbor residents who are also developing condominiums on the Marshall House property.

Additional hotels soon followed the original opening of the Marshall House — the Cliff House on Bald Head Cliff in the Cape Neddick region near the Ogunquit line, the Harmon House and Hotel Albracca in various parts of York Harbor, and the Sea Cottage at Long Beach, among others. A further impetus to growth was the opening of the York Harbor and York Beach Railroad Company as a branch of the Boston and Maine. Passengers arriving at York Harbor and Long Beach were met by livery teams from the hotels. Large expectations accompanied the building of the railroad, as the published comment of a booster, George Alexander Emery, suggests:

> Should the contemplated railroad be built in the right place and no endeavor be made to shun that portion of the town from which it would derive the most business, the trade with Boston and Portland now carried on by coasting vessels may be diverted to it. With such facilities of connection, no doubt, manufactories would also be established. Adding such advantages to the beauties nature has bestowed upon it, York might resume its place among the thriving towns in New England.

Although economic conditions in York never entirely fulfilled these predictions, it is undeniable that the town prospered. Around the turn of the century, many new hotels were added, particularly in the York Beach section — Young's Hotel, the Union Bluff House, the Fairmont Hotel, Katahdin House, and the Sea View Hotel, among others. In the decade between 1880 and 1890, property valuation in York increased by 70 percent, for a total of more than $1.2 million, nearly all of it in shorefront property.

A contemporary description characterizes the change in York in terms that closely approximate today's booming real estate development, while somehow epitomizing the end of the last century through the quaint expressions employed by Samuel Adams Drake, who wrote in 1891:

> But a serpent has entered this Eden. I found that even here farmers were selling off their land to capitalists by the hundred acres in a lump. One goodman's face expanded in a broad grin when he said that nobody wanted to buy his good land, but everybody was crazy after his poorest. They might have the 'veew' and welcome, he said, he would 'heave' that in . . . He wanted to know how prices were going at York and whether it was true that four acres had just been sold at Eastern Point for $16,000. In short, he had become a full-fledged land speculator, to whom his old occupation was already grown distasteful, and his smock frock a badge of servitude.

In 1889, York Beach acquired its first public amusement device, a "marine car" run on rails that carried passengers out to sea for an exhilarating ride. It was the invention of John E. Staples, later a State Representative, who operated it along with Samuel W. Junkins, an indefatigable early promoter of the resort. Next came St. Aspinquid Park, an amusement center owned and serviced by a streetcar line, and containing a casino, restaurant, menagerie, walks, carriage drives, and rustic arbors. (Even today, York Beach has its amusement park and a zoo, the Animal Forest Park.)

York's streetcar line, the Portsmouth, Dover and York St. Railway, or "Pull, Drag and Yank," was actually an amalgamation of several local lines. It was unique among New England street railways in operating a ferry which crossed the Piscataqua River between Portsmouth and Kittery. Before it could run to York Beach, the line had to defeat an injunction brought by York Harbor residents. A 1908 advertising brochure describes the scene along the way:

> Leaving the village, we pass the soldiers' monument . . . and then descend under the brow of Sentry Hill to York Harbor post office. The harbor is the mecca of wealthy people from all over the country and we pass many fine residences as the car climbs the hill that overlooks the harbor mouth and the bathing beach. The tract sloping east from the summit of the hill is called Norwood Farm and from here a fine view is had of Long Sands, the Nubble with its lighthouse and the wooded hills inland, Mount Agamenticus rising in the distance.
>   We pass along Long Beach siding and then follow the curving strand . . . The next siding is Sea Cottage and soon after leaving it, the track swerves inland and emerges at the western end of York Beach proper. On the bluff at the right is Concordville, while the hotels in the distance are on Union Bluff. Our car stops at the square within a minute's walk of the beach . . .

The advertising of York in those days featured not only the recreational and scenic aspects but also its potential as a health resort. An endorsement from F. D. Stackpole, M.D., declared that ". . . in my 15 years experience and practice here, I have never known a case of serious illness to originate here. Malaria and typhoid fever contracted elsewhere have speedily recovered here. In fact, I know of no place better situated for the cure of malaria . . ."

It was soon evident that resorts of two types were developing within the same community. York Harbor attracted the wealthy and socially prominent, in much the manner of Bar Harbor. The York Harborites hailed from such cities as Boston, New York, Philadelphia, and Washington, D.C. The summer visitors to York Beach came mainly from New Hampshire towns — Dover, Somersworth, Manchester, and Concord. Many of them, according to Ralph F. Lowe in an unpublished manuscript of remembrances, were mill workers and "such working people as could get away for a few weeks only. Indeed," he continues, ". . . the highways from Dover and the Berwicks would be jammed on Saturday nights with teams full of those coming to remain over Sunday. The most of these people were below middle class. From the Corner to the Village, one would think crowds were gathering for a gigantic fair." To York Harbor at the same time were coming such distinguished visitors as the young John Jacob Astor; Charles W. Eliot, president of Harvard; General Charles Devens; Maine Senator and U.S. Presidential candidate James G. Blaine; Susan Hale, the sister of Edward Everett Hale; Ole Bull, the Norwegian violinist; and Alice Longfellow, daughter of the poet. Her father and his contemporary, John Greenleaf Whittier, had both been summer visitors to York. The distinction that appeared, without deliberate planning, between the two sides of York's summer business — the one exclusive, the other popular — remains to this day.

By 1920, York's summer population was estimated at 16,000. By 1929, York had no less than 500 summer cottages and hotels. Ralph Lowe wrote, looking back in amazement: "The visitor of today at York Harbor can hardly believe how simple and plain the place was 80 years ago, before the modernization. There was not much communication with the outside world. The main business was fishing and farming."

Another sign of how much conditions have changed is Lowe's report that those earlier fishermen used lobsters *for bait* — whereas those taken from the waters off York today are all but worth their weight in gold.

Separation Sentiment Starts

But the sociological division between York Beach and York Harbor was not the only such development. Besides the two resorts, there was also the rest of York — "York Village," as it was called. Still more pronounced was the attitude of both waterfront communities, where most of the taxable property was to be found, toward the rest of the town, where most of the year-round population lived.

York had known sectional differences before this. First Parish and Second Parish were so distinct as almost to be separate communities. As long ago as 1828, in fact, Joseph Thompson and eighty others had petitioned the Legislature to authorize two towns, the area of the First Parish to be known as "East York" and that of the Second

Parish to be called, of all things, "New York." The lawmakers did not approve the plan.

In 1834, however, the same solons detached a section of the Tatnic region from northwest York and gave it to the town of South Berwick. But since most of the families living there gravitated toward South Berwick anyhow, the change seemed reasonable and was not resisted.

The long quarrel that developed around the turn of the century had to do with the use of tax money. The waterfront areas had the taxable property, and the other areas had the votes. Would the farmers on the "Mountain" at the western edge of York — the "Outer Commons" of colonial days — vote for improvements at York Beach and York Harbor? Presumably they would not. And indeed they did not.

In 1901, bills were presented to the seventieth Maine Legislature for setting up the York Beach Village Corporation and the York Harbor Village Corporation — an official device then commonly in use, by which a particular segment of a community governed itself, while remaining legally a part of the larger community. Through such legislation a corporation can be assured a percentage of the town's tax revenue. Independent services — such as police, and highway departments — can be established by the corporation. This has been done in York Beach and York Harbor. Other municipal expenses — such as schools — do not figure in the situation at York.

The York Beach corporation bill was presented on the petition of William H. Hogarth and others, and the York Harbor corporation bill on the petition of Wilson M. Walker and twenty-five others. Both bills were sponsored by John E. Staples, the Representative from York, and the inventor of the York Beach "marine car." Senator George E. Morrison of Saco pushed them through the Senate, while Staples dealt with the House. There was no opposition, no debate. The two bills were enacted on March 20 and March 21, 1901, and were subsequently signed by Gov. John F. Hill. They became effective after voters within the corporation boundaries met at special meetings called by certain citizens named in the legislation. In York Beach, William H. Hogarth, Will C. Hildreth, and R. F. Talpey were empowered to call the meeting. In York Harbor, those designated were William S.

Putnam, Joseph W. Simpson, Fremont Varrell, John H. Varrell, and Joseph C. Bridges.

The ease with which these village corporations were formed belied the tensions that were building in the town. Before the decade was over, these tensions were to become explosive.

The Bridge

In 1896, Edward B. Blaisdell, a prominent York architect and builder, expressed in a published statement his glowing optimism concerning the future of his native town: "Having witnessed the steady growth of York for the last 30 years, I can say it has grown on its own merits, as the place has never been boomed or advertised. It has never ceased growing a single year and is of more importance today than ever before. When I view York Harbor with its beautiful river, lovely islands and matchless bathing beach, York Beach with its beauty, York Cliffs with its rugged scenery, fine sea view and wooded background, it makes me feel proud to call it my birthplace."

Although it is doubtful that Blaisdell's enthusiasm ever flagged, less than a decade later he was to be the storm center of a controversy that nearly tore the town apart.

In 1905, the Selectmen of York asked the Legislature for authority to build a new highway and bridge that would link York Harbor with points to the south. The Legislature allowed the County Commissioners to lay out the way and the bridge, as petitioned by 186 York citizens. A public hearing was held on May 18, 1905, and on January 2, 1906, the Commissioners decided to proceed.

But opposition to the bridge had been gathering. The vote at a town meeting in October, 1906, was close — 174-123. The principal objection was the cost. York citizens who lived away from the shore believed the improvement would solely benefit the resort business. That one of the County Commissioners was none other than Samuel Junkins, the promoter of York Beach, was openly resented. The resentment grew fiercer when it was learned that he owned a quarter interest in Bragdon Island, through which the proposed way was to pass.

The political maneuvering now became intricate. A "Bridge Committee," to consist of the three selectmen

The Marine Car (c. 1890).
The first amusement device at York Beach,
built and promoted by John Staples,
who was later York's representative
in the State Legislature, and
Samuel Jenkins. Both men were
early pioneers in the tourist
business in York.

and four citizens, was approved by the town meeting. It also voted to accept Edward B. Blaisdell's bid to build the project for $30,000. The seven-member bridge committee soon dwindled to a committee of four, however, the selectmen having withdrawn once they decided to oppose the bridge. But the remaining members of the bridge committee awarded Blaisdell a contract for $39,500 to go ahead with the work.

Go ahead Blaisdell did, despite town meetings, federal government hearings, injunctions, mandamus proceedings, and other litigation. By March, 1908, Blaisdell had completed the project. But he hadn't been paid. A pro-bridge town treasurer, John Conant Stewart — a doctor, lawyer, and former state senator — had borrowed money to pay Blaisdell, arguably without authority. A new town treasurer, Edward E. E. Mitchell, decided to retrieve the sum. No checks were issued to Blaisdell, because no selectman would sign them. Needless to say, Blaisdell sued.

On March 11, 1908, the bridge committee wrote the selectmen that the bridge and highway had been completed and were open for traffic — and that $49,765.63 was still owing. A week later, the selectmen responded:

> We do not recognize your right or authority to act in any way relating to the way and bridge matter . . . or that you are authorized to accept any way or bridge in this Town, and for and in behalf of the Inhabitants of the Town of York . . . We do not understand that the Inhabitants of the Town of York have ever entered into any valid contract for the construction of said pretended way and bridge, or that you had any authority to do any act or thing whereby the Town might become liable in this matter . . .

The missive also contained an ominous warning to the bridge committee that "the responsibility therefor as we understand it, rests upon you individually."

Were the bridge and way public or were they not? When a tugboat belonging to the Piscataqua Navigation Company arrived to tow a group of barges that were waiting at a brickyard on the York River, the tugboat captain whistled in vain for the draw to be lifted. There was no draw tender. The company complained to the U.S. Secretary of War that navigation had been obstructed. The federal government descended on the York selectmen, ordering them to open the draw. They complied, but then proceeded to *chain it open!*

Now it was impossible to travel over the highway. Complaints next went to the County Commissioners that a public highway was being blocked. The selectmen were forced to unchain the draw. They had to appoint a new draw tender at the town's expense. Still, obstinately, they refused to pay Blaisdell until a decision by the Maine Supreme Court in 1913 ruled in the contractor's favor. The final bill was $51,066.71.

"Yorktown," "Gorges," and the Fight in the Legislature

The bridge controversy divided York into fiercely opposing camps. Pro-bridge and anti-bridge feelings were so strong as to spawn a movement to split York physically. In 1908, notice was served that a bill creating the municipal entity of "Yorktown" would be presented to the 74th Legislature. In general the pro-bridge people favored this separation and the anti-bridge people opposed it.

Viewed another way, the split was between a majority of the people who opposed breaking up the town and a powerful and influential minority who wanted independence. Edward S. Marshall, now owner of the Marshall House, was a prime mover for separation. So were such wealthy summer residents as the New York corporation lawyer Francis Lynde Stetson and the Virginia novelist, socialite, and diplomat, Thomas Nelson Page.

The battle in York began even before the legislative session. A pro-separation Republican, Albert Bragdon, president of the bank, was expected to seek his party's nomination for State Representative, and would undoubtedly win. Nomination was tantamount to election in a town where Democrats did not win, rarely ran, and indeed hardly dared even show themselves. But the feeling against separation ran so deep that word now went out that if Bragdon ran, the anti-separation champion, Josiah Chase, although a Republican himself, would run on the Democratic ticket. There were also broad hints of a run on the bank. This threat was actually carried out, and it took a timely infusion of dollars by Edward S. Marshall and his friends to retrieve the situation. But the perhaps even direr threat, that York might have a Democratic Representative in the State Legislature, was averted. Party leaders talked Bragdon into withdrawing, and Chase went to Augusta as a Republican.

The pro-separation forces still had a potent spokesman, however, in Frank G. Marshall, son of Edward S. Marshall, who occupied a seat in the House as a State Representative from Portland. As the lines were drawn for a struggle between Frank Marshall and Josiah Chase, Chase seemed to have the advantage. He was the town's own Representative. He could offer petitions to prove that a large majority of the townspeople opposed "An Act Dividing the Town of York and Establishing Yorktown." In cases involving quarrels within towns, legislators usually like to side with the local Representative.

And the initial conclusion of the Towns Committee, after a grueling, six-and-a-half-hour public hearing that went on until 10:30 p.m., was almost unanimously negative. They reported six members against the bill, only one member for it. The holdout, however, was the committee chairman, Senator Patrick Theriault of Grand Isle. Why a legislator from the extreme northern tip of Maine should have been interested in the problems of a town at the state's southern extreme is best left to conjecture. Theriault not only supported the bill; he submitted a new draft proposing new boundaries and a new name, "Gorges," among other revisions intended to make the measure palatable.

It was a tactic of proponents to show that the new Theriault bill was a measure "everyone could live with." Senator Benjamin F. Hamilton of Dayton, who represented York County (senatorial districts then coincided with county lines) led off with this same pitch — that the new bill was a better one, which he was able to support — explaining, "Under this division, the new town's a seashore town. Their interests are different from the interests of the rural districts, vastly different. As you all understand, they want a great deal done and they are willing to pay for what they want done . . ." The new town, Hamilton explained, would include both village corporations formed eight years earlier. "These corporations," he said, "were organized there for self-defense."

Hamilton also brought in the bridge controversy. "They have a bridge over there that cost them $50,000 and that bridge is not paid for. That bridge caused a great deal of trouble. Now this new town proposes to take that bridge and pay for it."

The vote in the Senate to establish the Town of Gorges was 24-5.

Now it was the turn of the House. Again and again, during extended debate, the point was made of the willingness, nay, the eagerness, of the new town's citizenry to pay for services within their bailiwick. "These people who come there for summer resort are worth their millions and they want many improvements. They do not care how many improvements are made or how much it costs, but they want the money which they give to be laid out in improvements there, while those in the rural districts are opposed to this, so that their interests have not been identical."

It was also argued that these same summer people were leaving because they were disgruntled, business was at a standstill, and property values were depreciating.

Frank Marshall made a plea to the members' sense of history: "I think it would be well for the State of Maine to give one honorable monument to Sir Ferdinando Gorges who did so much to found the State of Maine."

Josiah Chase countered with a devastating forecast of what creating the town of Gorges would to to York. It would, he said "take away the high school, both grammar schools, a large part of the primary school, the town hall, the poor farm, the old jail museum, all the records of the town of York, the whole hydrant system, every U.S. post office, eight of the ten churches, two-thirds of the population and nearly two-thirds of the valuation." Conversely, while it would take 35 miles of road, it would leave York with no less than 105 miles to maintain. The valuation figures would give rich Gorges $2,130,000 and poor old York $370,000.

But Chase failed to touch enough responsive hearts. On the first vote, his plea was rejected almost three to one, in a tally of 93-35. From then on, the history of the bill consisted of attempts by Chase to attach various amendments providing for a referendum. One of these was resisted because it would have allowed women to vote;[9] somewhat less shocking, but no less acceptable, was another that would have permitted non-resident summer home owners to vote. By a heroic effort, Chase managed to tack on a clause empowering the selectmen to call for a vote. The pro-separationists, fearing that either the selectmen would never issue the call or, if they did, the vote would go against them, had this provision removed in the Senate. Back in the House, the crucial question was whether it could also be removed there. During this debate, a York County Representative, Moore of Saco, voiced aloud his suspicions about the puzzling strength of the pro-separation forces: "Who is prompting this? A lobby, a paid lobby, which has been here all winter, all winter long, trafficking and tying people up on this proposition to divide the town of York"

A powerful lobby it was, without doubt. Chase's amendment lost once again 69-58. On April 1, 1909, the bill was enacted, and shortly afterward signed into law.

Why, then, did no town of Gorges come into being as an "honorable monument" to the man "who did so much to found the State of Maine?"

The reason lies in the continued strenuous exertions of Josiah Chase, along with those of George F. Plaisted, the Town Clerk, and the many York citizens who rallied to take advantage of the new provision in Maine law for an "initiative" under which a sufficient number of petitions could place a question on a statewide ballot. The York Referendum Association actually gathered 13,000 signatures, a number that was deemed sufficient after official scrutiny (64 signatures by inmates of the Portland jail were disallowed). The Governor put the proposition before the electorate. Edward S. Marshall vowed to spend $100,000 on the campaign, and the people of Maine were treated to more of the same spectacle that had consumed so much legislative time in 1909 — namely, the internal squabbles of the town of York.

---

[9] This observation was made, perhaps tongue in cheek, by Rep. William R. Pattangall, later Chief Justice of the Maine Supreme Court. Pattangall was a noted wit, nicknamed the "Mark Twain of Maine," and author of a series of famed satirical political sketches, "The Meddybemps Letters."

A magazine article went so far as to intimate that the subject would have national ramifications, particularly in national Republican politics. The writer wasn't specific, except to say that ex-Governor John F. Hill (who signed the York Beach and York Harbor Corporation bills) was a member of the Republican National Committee, and that Maine voted first in national elections, going to the polls in September rather than November. John F. Hill, incidently, was a native of nearby Eliot and an officer of the streetcar line that served York Beach.

The citizens of Maine voted overwhelmingly to keep York whole, a total of 31,722 to 19,692. In York itself the vote was 436 to 90. And so the town of Gorges, as proposed by Edward S. Marshall, John Conant Stewart, Francis Lynde Stetson, Thomas Nelson Page, and the rest, became a "might-have-been" of history.

The 250th Anniversary Celebration

A further dimension is added to all this if we go back a few years to what was undoubtedly the biggest celebration in York's history — the show put on for the town's 250th birthday, as dated from its incorporation as a town under Puritan Massachusetts in 1652.

Although in the year 1902, York had not as yet been racked by the Gorges controversy, its division into village corporations had already occurred. Nevertheless the distinguished speakers could and did speak of York as a single community, glorious in its past, blessed in its future prospects.

These distinguished speakers included, in addition to Francis Lynde Stetson and Thomas Nelson Page — who seemed always to be on hand where York affairs were concerned — ex-Governor Joshua Chamberlain, a Civil War general and hero at Gettysburg; James Phinney Baxter, a distinguished former mayor of Portland, now appearing as president of the Maine Historical Society; Thomas Brackett Reed, a former Speaker of the U.S. House of Representatives; and the incomparable Mark Twain, author, raconteur, and summer resident . . .

The world little notes nor long remembers what is said on such ceremonial occasions — even when a record is printed, as it was for this one. In view of what happened afterward in York, it is amusing to hear Francis Lynde

Stetson assure his audience: "Not despondency but hope is justified by the record of our past progress, and by our present conditions. At your next great feast of commemoration the sons and daughters of York surely shall declare that here, and in New England, life is not only true, but that it is also interesting . . ."

It seems unlikely that the New York corporation lawyer was prophet enough to have used the word "interesting" in the sense implied by the Chinese curse, "May you live in interesting times."

As for Thomas Nelson Page — Virginian, friend of Woodrow Wilson, future ambassador to Italy, author of *The Old South, The Old Dominion,* and *Robert E. Lee; Man and Soldier,* among many other books with a Southern point of view — the speech he made to the York celebration expressed pleasure at being asked to participate ("It shows my interest in York — my virtue as a citizen of York — was understood"), referred to "coming as I do from an old house on the banks of another York River in another colony planted by the same people," but above all offered some strangely Populist sentiments concerning the inequality of wealth in the U.S. and of the political corruption that went with it:

> Wealth piles up in the central marts. The power of organizations is so tremendous that it brings about vast aggregations of capital, till it is said that the inequality is such that one third of one per cent of the population own seventy per cent of the entire property of the country in value . . . This would matter little if with wealth did not go hand in hand corruption — not mere personal corruption — but corruption by organization, corruption of the fountain heads of legislation of justice.

Odd words from an establishment figure in Republican York. One wonders what the Republican leader Thomas Brackett Reed was thinking. Certainly, everyone in the audience looked forward to hearing Tom Reed. His reputation as a wit was unsurpassed. In 1896, a Republican rally in York featuring Tom Reed had drawn five thousand people. Many stories were told of this giant of a man, 300 pounds, 6 feet 3, who had represented York's Congressional district in Washington and had ruled from

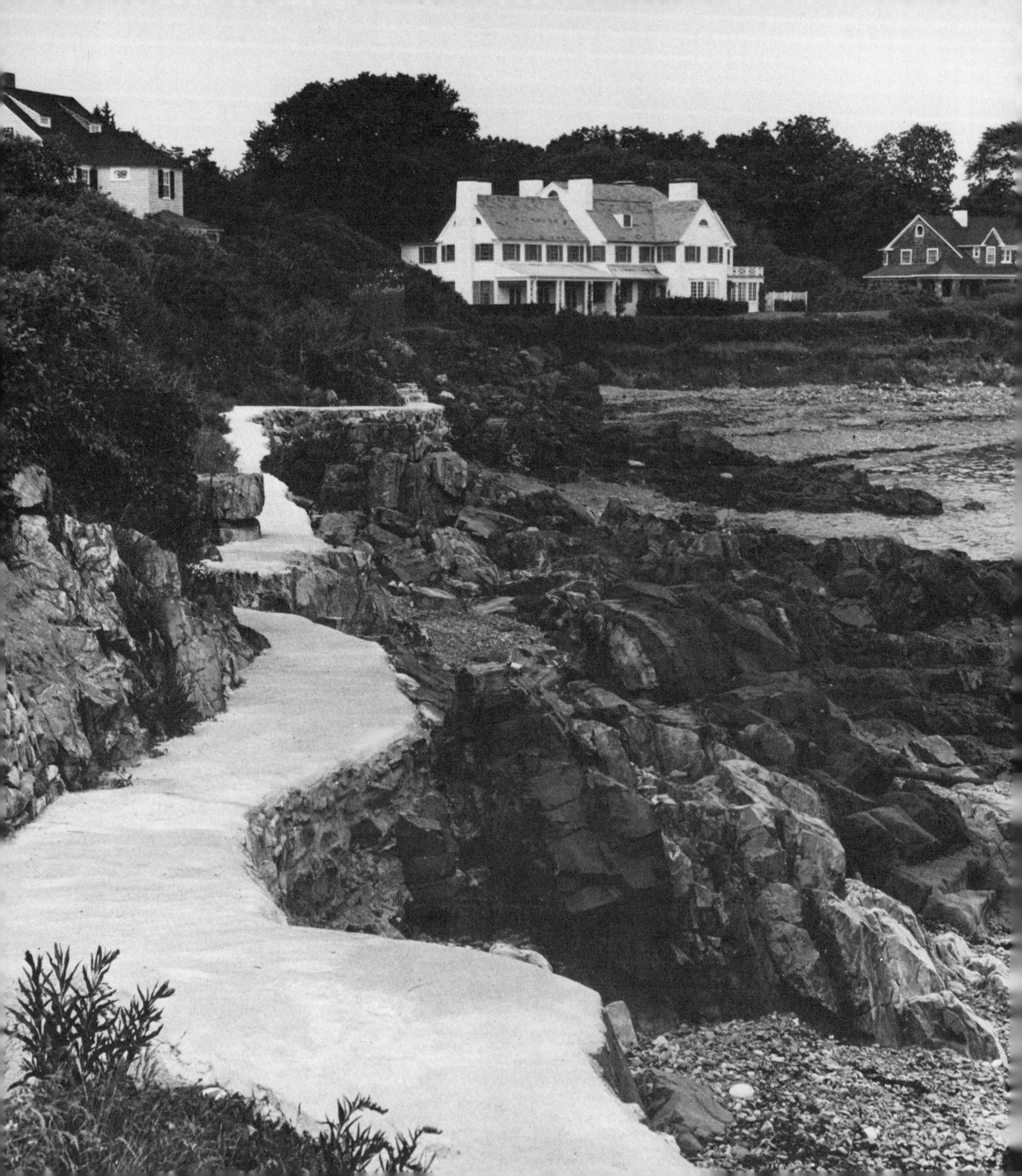

the Speaker's chair with more power than any presiding officer before or since. Reed's quips were famous. "All the wisdom in the world consists in shouting with the majority," was one; "A Statesman is a politician who is dead," was another. When a declaiming Congressman declared he would rather be right than President, Reed replied, "The gentleman need not be disturbed. He will never be either." When a Congressman began, as he addressed the Chair, "I was thinking, Mr. Speaker. I was thinking . . ." Reed shot back, "No one will interrupt the gentleman's commendable innovation." To a Representative from Massachusetts he said, "Russell, you do not understand the theory of five-minute debate. The object is to convey to the House either information or misinformation. You have consumed several periods of five minutes this afternoon without doing either." Reed once said of two colleagues, "They never open their mouths without subtracting from the sum of human knowledge." Another time, Reed took note of a victim he had just left speechless by declaring, "Having embedded that fly in the liquid amber of my remarks, I will proceed."

It is regrettable that a mere summary is all that remains of Reed's comments on this occasion. Possibly he was not in good form in this twilight phase of his career. His dry, droll Maine humor did come across in the recorded allusions to his ancestral ties with York.[10] "Mr. Reed said that by looking upon the programme, and finding his name not enrolled there, one might consider his presence an intrusion were it not for the fact that his ancestors came from York, although so far as he could learn they never occupied any high position of trust. In fact he had hard work to discover they ever existed; and certainly they held no position of great emolument, judging from his financial condition when he arrived."

Mark Twain, the final speaker, was whimsical, charming, good-humoredly satirical. He began by saying that "he had come to York to instruct it in its ancient history, to rectify the morals of its inhabitants and to otherwise do valuable things in the way of didactics." He then announced that he had just received a letter from the audience signed "One of the Victims," stating "that there had

The Marginal Way.
This walkway along the ocean is open to the public.

---

[10] He was also a descendant of one of the earliest seventeenth-century Maine settlers, George Cleaves.

never been any but the best weather until he (Twain) had come to York, and seemed to place the blame entirely on him, demanding that he either apologize or go away." He might do the first, Twain said, but he flatly refused the latter. "In thirty-seven days he had had no fault to find with the weather as he had stayed strictly at home, and the rain seemed to come only when it thought it could catch one out. For thirty-four of the thirty-seven days he had worked, and that was something he never before had been able to do. The climate, he thought, prevented moral deterioration, for he had worked four Sundays without breaking the Sabbath." He then went on with some inspired nonsense about matches:

> One of the most serious questions with which he had to contend in York was matches. If he wished to smoke, it was next to impossible to get a light. He could buy only a sort of match with a picture of the inventor on each box and labeled "Safety." He felt free to say that they are so safe one cannot light them. Even Satan, the inventor and a distant relative of his, can't use them for he has no appliances to make them go, and is utilizing them to build cold storage vaults for such choice morsels as Voltaire, Benjamin Franklin, Alexander VI; and he has a wistful eye on some other notables not yet started — and here present!"

Twain also joked about the town's profusion of post offices. ". . . York Cliffs, York Beach, York Harbor, York Village, York Corner and so on. In fact, one cannot throw a brickbat across a thirty-seven-acre lot without danger of disabling a postmaster; they are thick as aldermen in the days of the old city charter." America's favorite humorist concluded by saying that "if he stayed here he expected to attend York's tricentennial in fifty years, for already he had grown younger by many years than he was on his arrival."

Some Literary Allusions

There were other literary visitors to York in Twain's time, just as there had been in the time of Whittier and Longfellow. Sarah Orne Jewett, undoubtedly the finest writer Maine has ever produced, lived in nearby South

Berwick, and frequently came to York. The poet Celia Thaxter, on her island off the coast of Kittery, attracted other cultural notables. William Dean Howells, famed as a novelist and editor, has been more commonly associated with Kittery Point, but also appears to have been counted as a York resident, and was on the stand with Mark Twain at the 250th Anniversary celebration. Booth Tarkington was often in York. A book on Maine by Henry E. Dunnack, the state librarian, published in 1920, asserted: "There are the numerous authors of distinction, literally colonies of them in some instances, notably at York Harbor and Kennebunkport, who have established vacation homes in Maine and who come here summer after summer. If we can count them neither as native writers nor as adopted sons and daughters of Maine, we can at least point in almost every case to the direct influence of Maine on their writings."

Maybe, though the thesis would be hard to prove. There is a Maine short story by Thomas Nelson Page, entitled "Miss Godwin's Inheritance," which extolled the "virtues of the countryside as opposed to the stifling atmosphere of the city" and told of a girl's efforts to restore her grandfather's summer home. "Leander Light," another of Page's Maine stories, concerns an old man who refuses to sell his summer home to a speculator, but leaves it instead to the town for a hospital or school, thus rebuking the vulgar materialism of the new generation. New England provides the setting of yet another Page story, "My Friend, the Doctor." However, the Virginian's more substantial works such as *Red Rock, Red Riders, On Newfound River* — none of which is now remembered — are stories set in the South.

But Page was part of a group that had a lasting influence on York. These were the members of a York Harbor social club, the Reading Room — so called perhaps because it did have a somewhat literary flavor, or perhaps because the title happened to be fashionable at the time (Bar Harbor had its Reading Room). The club is still in existence, and still maintains a certain aura of exclusivity. Founded in 1897, it was primarily envisioned, according to Humphrey T. Nichols, one of the charter members, as a place where gentlemen could gather to drink and talk in pleasant, convivial surroundings. It was not until May 29, 1910, that the club moved into its present quarters and began to admit women — an innovation that many members mistakenly forecast would spell its doom, though it definitely brought to an end the informality of earlier days. As Nichols recalls the Reading Room's inception on July 4, 1897, "The members, stripped to their undershirts, whitewashed the little wooden picket fence in front of the clubhouse — repairing to the kitchen every now and again to partake of the 'Fish House' punch."

Nichols further remembers nostalgically that "the talk was of the best — ranging from most disastrous chances of moving accidents by flood and field, of hair-breadth 'scapes i' the imminent deadly breach, to sparkling anecdotes and brilliant interchange of wit and repartee . . . Art, Science, Politics and Religion — each and all received due attention. It was a rare privilege to join this little circle and to listen, spellbound, to its infinite variety."

The best known literary figure to play an active role in the York Harbor Reading Room was Finley Peter Dunne, satirist, newspaperman, and creator of "Mr. Dooley," the philosophical Irishman whose pungent comments in phonetic brogue on the state of American politics earned him a permanent place in American letters. Nichols recalls how Dunne, with typical irreverence "avowed that he would never be satisfied until he had written a York Harbor novel — its hero to be named 'Mons. Veneris' and his heroine 'Albracca Garage.' And he called our Club 'The Reeling Room.'" Dunne, it might be added, was official taster of the fish house punch.

Nichols himself is described as a "wit, raconteur, poet, and author of appropriate phrases in classical Latin." Other literary figures connected with the club include the authors Arthur C. Smith, John Fox, Jr., and Robert Herrick. But the Reading Room's most enduring contribution to York and, indeed, to a much wider geographical area, was not literary. Louise Dickinson Rich, herself an able writer, observes in *The Coast of Maine, An Informal History:* "There wasn't much reading done in the Reading Room. It was really the equivalent of the old country store, where the citizens met to talk things over while killing time. Out of this talk grew the York Harbor Village Corporation and the zoning ordinances which the Corporation sponsored. This was probably the first instance of zoning in New England, and certainly in Maine."

Another and still better known Maine writer, Kenneth Roberts has told of this pioneer effort in *Trending Into Maine*. The author of *Northwest Passage* records how the campaign for zoning began as a response of the Corporation officials to the threat of expanding tourist accommodations on York's easterly outskirts posed by what were known as Libby Camps,[11] which he declared with undisguised snobbery had "spread with such fungus-like rapidity" that York Harbor "was in danger of being almost completely swamped by young ladies in shorts, young men in soiled undershirts and fat ladies in knickerbockers . . ."

He tells in some detail how the initial law divided York Harbor into residential, business, and limited business zones; how it provided for the replacement of combustible roofs with noncombustible shingles; how it restricted stores, shops, hot dog stands, and public garages to certain localities, required building permits, and forbade billboards.

Before the law was enacted, the battle went to the Maine Supreme Court. York Harbor won, with a ruling that the zoning statutes and ordinances were constitutional. Kenneth Roberts hailed the decision as an accomplishment of the Reading Room: "As a result of the long, long fight of the wise men who founded and maintained the York Harbor Reading Room, York Harbor will always be one of Maine's outstanding resorts and proudest possessions, a delight to everyone who goes there . . ."

York can claim yet another distinction as the birthplace of America's first female novelist, Sally Sayward Barrell. A granddaughter of Jonathan Sayward, the Tory judge, and a daughter of Nathaniel Barrell, the unexpected supporter of the Constitution, she came to be known after several marriages, one of them to General Abiel Wood, as "Madam Wood" and under that name achieved a fleeting fame in American letters. She also wrote under such pen names as "A Lady of Maine," or "A Lady of Massachusetts." Among her works, which began appear-

---

[11] This summer camping area, populated by mobile homes and founded by a gentleman named Libby, is still being used in York.

ing soon after 1800, were *Julia and the Illuminated Baron, Dorval or the Speculator, Amelia,* and *Tales of Night.* Madam Wood early preached development of "American" literature, rather than a slavish copying of English style — even though, paradoxically, her most ambitious works were not set in America. She did enunciate a philosophy, however: "Why should we not aim at independence, with respect to our mental enjoyments, as well as for our more substantial gratifications, I know not. Why must the amusements of our leisure hours cross the Atlantic? and introduce foreign fashions and foreign manners, to a people certainly capable of producing their own."

A recently rediscovered short story by Madam Wood does have an American setting, close to her native York and to her own family experience. Entitled "War, the Parent of Domestic Calamity — A Tale of the Revolution," it takes place primarily in New Hampshire, and concerns a Tory family whose daughter is in love with a Revolutionary hero. Everyone dies — Tory and Patriot alike — and everyone is noble, so as to bring home the tragedy of civil conflict. Although the writing is bad and the plot atrocious, the story is intriguing for its sympathetic treatment of the Tory point of view which Madam Wood found a natural one. And she begins her tale with an expression of understanding, if not gratitude, for the less than dire treatment of her own Tory forebears:

> It would be proof of apathy which the sons and daughters of sentiment and patriotic feelings would not wish to profess were an American to peruse the annals of his country with a conscious pride that so few sanguinary acts have been committed, so little blood has been shed in the revolutionary war, that the page of the historian had been so seldom sullied by recitals from which the eye turns with disgust and the heart sickens to contemplate.

Madam Wood in later years wrote some non-fiction "Reminiscences," which touched on local York history. An example was her treatment of the "sixteen silver porringers," reputedly sent to York from Canada by her own Sayward relative, Mother Superior Sister Marie-des-Anges. These porringers were a gift from the former

Esther Sayward to her sixteen Yankee nieces and nephews whom she had never seen. One nephew — the famous Jonathan, Madam Wood's grandfather — characteristically bought up the other fifteen, then had them all melted into six large porringers.

Fiction about York itself is rare. But in 1878, Edward P. Tenney wrote a novel, *Agamenticus,* based directly on the town's history — a treatment of Samuel Moody's successful effort to convert York from a sinful refuge of godless non-Puritan backwoodsmen and fisher folk into a more conventional, godly, and upright New England town. Tenney says in an introduction:

> Historians agree that Agamenticus was settled by adventurers — many of them reckless and licentious — refugees and outlaws from neighboring colonies and from Europe; that their first preachers were little better than their people; that near the close of the 17th Century, religious motives obtained little hold on the major part of the population; that scenes of merry-making and brutal life greeted Samuel Moody when he first settled in the wilderness — but before his death the wild country blossomed as the rose.

Tenney, who had high hopes for his work, explains in an afterword that he included no footnotes on historical matters within the body of his narrative because to break in with footnotes would be no less appropriate than to interrupt Dante. "If *Agamenticus* ever becomes as famous as *Inferno* and *Paradiso,*" he pledged, "it will appear in an octavo with three volumes of footnotes."

In the story, Pastor Moody appears as the Reverend David Benson. His wife is a Sewall, and his oldest son, Sewall Benson, takes the role of "Handkerchief Moody" in the real-life story. Sewall Benson, nicknamed "Quog" (other Benson children are "Quill" and "Crow"), kills his best friend, George Preble, in a hunting accident and later dons the black veil that Hawthorne made famous. A section of Agamenticus where the younger Benson eventually goes to preach is the wicked abode of "Firetown." The elder Benson, against a background of historic events including the Norridgewock and Louisbourg campaigns, eventually accomplishes his purpose.

In this healthy Agamenticus climate, it is of no consequence that two-thirds of the soil is incapable of cultivation, if the crops of children raised here have so much care bestowed upon them as is needed for their development . . . The little family burial lots upon farms, with white or brown headstones, all over this quaint town, are more precious legacies than the mines of Peru, if the memory of the just is blessed to the children. Hay and eggs and children are the chief products and exports of modern Agamenticus. David Benson's mark is on the children, and they are welcome in all markets . . .

Tenney, although not an exceptional writer, occasionally produces a striking descriptive passage. Particularly good, with an air of authenticity as to what York must have been like, is his thumbnail portrait of two volunteer warriors about to set sail for Louisbourg:

Bill Herke and Tom Ryan — who were firm friends, having been often drunk together — both enlisted. They had one shirt between them; it was changed faithfully every Sunday morning, each wearing it a week, but it was allowed no rest for a washing day. Tom wore a sort of eel-pot hat made of rushes; his beard — filthy with tobacco juice and beer drippings — reached far down upon his breast. Bill had a decidedly "bunged up" look about the eye, one being closed, the other cocked. His nose was a mere bob; his mouth a slit, from which a puff of smoke issued, and his chin looked like a peeled onion.

Moralizing at the end of his book, the author suggests how York's experience can be related to the rest of the world: "The hearty, homely zeal and love and practical sense of men like David Benson were never more needed than today . . . It must be acknowledged that the power which, under God, transformed Agamenticus is the most beneficent the world has seen, and that the introduction of like power into every community is the way to bring in the perfect age."

The Norridgewock raid by York soldiers figures in a narrative poem of John Greenleaf Whittier's, "Mogg

Megone," a gruesome tale that the Quaker poet later repudiated. He wrote on March 18, 1857, ". . . that the long poem of Mogg Megone was, in a great measure, composed in early life . . . its subject is not such as the writer would have chosen at any subsequent period." It is extremely vivid, nevertheless, — filled with the sound and sight of battle and the terror inspired by Johnson Harmon and Jeremiah Moulton, the mighty Indian fighters from York, as these excerpts suggest:

> A footstep — is it the step of Cleaves;
> With Indian blood on his English sword?
> Steals Harmon down from the sands of York
> With hand of iron and foot of cork?
>
> For Bomazeen from Tacconock
> Has sent his runners to Norridgewock,
> With tidings that Moulton and Harmon of York
> Far up the river have come.
> They have left their boats — they have entered the wood,
> and filled the depths of the solitude
> With the sound of the ranger's drum.
>
> The bark of dogs — the squaw's mad scream
> the dash of paddles along the stream —
> The whistle of shot as it cuts the leaves
> Of the maples around the church's eaves —
> And the gride of hatchets, fiercely thrown
> On wigwam log and tree and stone.
>
> Silent, the Indian points his hand
> To where across the echoing glen
> Sweep Harmon's dreaded ranger-band
> And Moulton with his men.
>
> No wigwam smoke is curling there:
> The very earth is scorched and bare:
> And they pause and listen to catch a sound
> Of breathing life — but there comes not one,
> Save the fox's bark and the rabbit's bound,
> But here and there on the blackened ground,
> White bones are glistening in the sun.

The most famous of all literary works associated with York is "Maud Muller, A Ballad" another of Whittier's long poems. Supposedly written in York Harbor in the 1870's while Whittier was visiting his sister Elizabeth, it ranks close to such well-known works as "Barbara Frietchie" and "Snowbound." Whittier thought little of it; his sister sent the poem to his publisher. Legend has it that he stopped at Samuel Smith's spring in the Brixham district of the York countryside, just beyond the Grange Hall, and inquired the way of a barefoot farm girl, Mary Smith, who wore a broad-brimmed hat, and who self-consciously raked hay over her feet as they talked. Near Smith's spring, which still gushes with pure water, there is now a stone tablet inscribed with a couplet recalling the poet's moment of inspiration:

> She stooped where the cool spring bubbled up
> And filled for him her small tin cup.

This meeting with the farmer's daughter led Whittier to imagine a chance encounter between "Maud Muller" (the surname came from Whittier's hometown of Haverhill, Massachusetts) and an unnamed judge:

> Maud Muller, on a summer's day,
> Raked the meadow sweet with hay.
> Beneath her torn hat glowed the wealth
> Of simple beauty and rustic health.

Each one dreams of what it might be like to be married to the other. They go their separate ways, he marrying a snob, she a rural clod, but continue to think of each other:

> Alas for maiden, alas for Judge,
> For rich repiner and household drudge!
> God pity them both! and pity us all
> Who vainly the dreams of youth recall.

> For all sad words of tongue or pen,
> the saddest are these: "It might have been!"

Many years later, with tongue decidedly in cheek, a local poet produced another version of "Maud Muller."

Edward E. Young, a businessman of Sentry Hill, York Harbor, ended his *Poetical Works* with a work that is presented here in its entirety. Its irreverence is not necessarily typical of native York humor, but neither is it entirely atypical.

> Maud Muller on a summer's day
> Was in a hammock on the front porch
> The Judge (came) up in his new Ford car
> And asked her if she could tell him
> Where he could get a drink.
> She said she could let him have a drink
> If he would hold his tongue about it.
> And the Judge got a drink.
> The Judge married a rich woman
> Who took the best automobile he had
> And ran away with the chauffeur.
> Maud Muller married a bootlegger
> And always had plenty of money.
> But she never had any children
> To be playing round her door.
> She would not be bothered with them.
> Of all sad words of tongue or pen
> The saddest are these: The Judge will
> Never see his nice automobile again.

In Conclusion

A book could still be written about what has been left out of this account. In fact, several such books are already in existence. The present effort has been primarily to depict a community, much as a novelist would depict a character.

But the author is painfully aware of how much he omitted. The history of education in York, and the development of its religious institutions have not received detailed attention. Many families whose members figure in the history of the town have not been cited. Such famed of ill-famed local characters — as Joanne Ford, notorious in the 17th century, the recipient of nine stripes of the whip for calling the Constable a "hornheaded, cowheaded rogue," or as, in a later age, Hepzibah "Hip" Cane and Polly Austin, two female hermits whose wild appearance infallibly attracted droves of children, or Dinah, the cantankerous slave woman of "Dinah's Hill," or "Johnny

Candlestrip," another hermit, or other still living eccentrics who are thus better left unmentioned — might have enlivened these pages with a few colorful details.

York has had its share of genuine rogues, "cow-headed" or otherwise. Mentioned earlier was the adulterous Rev. George Burdett, who around 1640 came to York after being driven out of Dover, New Hampshire, and then was shipped off to England after three convictions. In 1721 a spurious mining stock promotion scheme was foisted upon the town by the aptly named Caleb Spurrier. In 1866, at least one York citizen, Johnson B. Moulton, fell victim to the delusion of "George Washington Adams" and his "Lost Colony" Palestine Emigration Association, which left some 156 Maine citizens stranded in Palestine. Mark Twain was aboard the luxury steamer *Quaker City* which picked up most of the survivors after they had been, as Twain put it, "so shamefully humbugged by their prophet." In more recent times, the promotion of a purported "oceanographic school," at the former Emerson Hotel in York Harbor, was looked at askance by local authorities.

No Yankee town would be complete without its witch. York has the grave of one, according to local reputation. She was Mary Nason, wife of Samuel Nason, or Nasson,[12] and died August 28, 1772, rather late in the day for a witch. There was also, in more recent times, a gentleman whose will stipulated that champagne bottles in stone were to be placed on his grave — which they were, until because of the press of sightseers to the grave and the complaints that ensued, his widow had them removed.

Thousands of amusing human interest stories could be told about York — from the "cow caught on the cod hook" brand of rural buffoonery, or more famed incidents like the horseback ride of General Jeremiah McIntyre "up onto the second story of his home after his returning from a particularly boisterous muster," to others more sophisticated. There was the time a water tower was built behind an exquisite church on the Shore Road, so disrupting the view that York voters demanded the

---

[12] Reputedly for whom Nasson College, a contemporary liberal arts school in Springvale, Maine, was named.

tower's removal despite substantial cost to the municipally controlled Water District.

The history of York Hospital deserves a chapter — beginning with the fund-raising party given in 1905 by Mrs. Newton Perkins, with Baron Komura of Japan and Count Serge Witte of Russia, delegates to the Russo-Japanese Peace Conference then being held in Portsmouth, among the contributors toward purchasing the Davidson estate as the hospital's site. The history of Nubble Light, another landmark, is already the subject of a pamphlet. Authorized by Congress in 1837, it was not actually built until 1879. The York Customs Office, gone since 1913, was another local feature that lasted for more than a century. Most Maine towns have volunteer fire departments. Some even have two, and York is one of those. In addition, there are the Redshirts, an auxiliary composed of wealthy summer fire buffs who meet annually at the Reading Room to raise funds for York's firefighters.

York's politics have figured here and there in this narrative. There was also the visit of President James Monroe to York in 1817 — the only one by a U.S. president. Andrew Jackson almost came, but took sick in Boston and never arrived. The town's post-civil War Republicanism has already been noted. The story is told of how, after Governor Garcelon, a Democrat, finished his speech on a visit to York, G.O.P. wags drove up to transport him home — in a hearse! The author's preference is for the tale of a lone Democrat who to celebrate Cleveland's victory in 1884, because "there weren't enough Democrats in town to organize a parade," bought gunpowder, lit a bonfire in back of his house, and invited all the boys in town to bring their shotguns and fire away all night long. The author's preference will be understood when it is explained that he is York's first Democratic Representative to the State Legislature — another sign of change in the old town, which some, I'm sure, would call a harbinger of "decline."

Today old political battles continue to be fought. A referendum on the question of abolishing the Village Corporations was approved by the 106th Maine Legislature for balloting on November 6, 1973, but failed to win by the required two-thirds majority. Meanwhile, a Charter Commission has begun drafting a charter for the town.

That a community with the distinction of being the first chartered city in America should have existed as a town for so long without a charter is perhaps more curious than ironic.

York's part in the temperance movement, and the genesis of Prohibition with the passage of the "Maine Law" in 1852, is another piece to be fitted into the historical jigsaw puzzle. National Prohibition and the smuggling of liquor along the York coast during this century are subjects on which much word-of-mouth material could be collected.

A darker subject still to be explored is York's part, if any, in the Ku Klux Klan craze that swept Maine during the early 1920s, when hooded figures, fueled by anti-Catholicism, marched throughout the State. Crime in York, and the drug problem that came there as to so many American communities in the turbulent sixties, are other less-than-pleasant subjects.

York is not a finished product. Community history did not stop with the decision in 1909 not to split the town into two municipalities. There is still drama in York's daily life — sometimes muted, sometimes harsh. The process of development still goes on.

There was the re-creation in 1970 of the York Militia as a ceremonial organization. A number of such colonial units already existed in Massachusetts, Connecticut, and elsewhere, but the newly constituted "York Militia Company" was the first of its kind in Maine. Governor Kenneth M. Curtis designated it the "Governor's Ceremonial Foot Guards" and as Maine's representative at the annual Patriot's Day Celebration in Concord, Massachusetts. The Militia Muster, held in York in August, almost overnight became a statewide tourist event, drawing thousands of visitors and upward of forty militia companies from as far away as New Jersey and New York State.

In the same spirit York's historical societies have taken an active part in trying to protect what remains of the past, and York's historical museums annually draw many visitors. In August, 1973, the National Park Service of the U.S. Department of the Interior approved the formation of the York Historic District, covering the center of York Village and York Harbor. The York District is now listed in the National Register of Historic Places as "a sweeping panorama of one of the most historically significant areas in our nation."

Each of the different components of the town — Cape Neddick, Scituate, Scotland, Brixham, Seabury, Birch Hill, Godfrey's Cove, Clay Hill, Cider Hill, Bay Haven, North Village — mentioning only some of the neighborhoods into which York is subdivided, has its story and deserves a chapter to itself — as do the now-vanished basket makers of the Mountain. Nothing less could begin to convey the subjective richness of particular scenes within the town — the sight of mallards rising from the Mill Pond; the flow of the tide beneath that swaying pedestrian thoroughfare, the Wiggily Bridge; the panorama of wet rocks, spray, and sea birds from the Marginal Way, the public walk skirting the large estates in York Harbor; fall foliage spread out below the fire watch tower on Mount Agamenticus (with its ski resort, which I almost forgot to mention); the absolute quiet of Bell Marsh; the white steeples and housetops seen from Sewall's Hill; or sunset from the wooden pilings of Sewall's Bridge, the oldest structure of its kind in America; the pristine beauty of the marshes in Brave Boat Harbor; the excitement of the crowded throngs at York Beach . . .

York in the final quarter of the twentieth century hardly faces the secure future that the speakers at the 1902 celebration so confidently forecast. Somehow, it must meet the impact of rapid change. For the town is growing with extraordinary speed. The 1970 census put its population at 5,500. Three years later, the figure had risen to 8,000. York is acquiring a new character — no longer that of a frontier outpost, a rural idyl, a fashionable retreat for the rich, or a middle-class summer resort, but of a bedroom community as the megalopolis of Greater Boston spreads northward. The challenge to York, as its thoughtful citizens acknowledge, is that of dealing with its new identity while holding on to the virtues of the past and the blessings of nature that still remain.

In 1874, a century ago, Nathaniel G. Marshall addressed his fellow townspeople in a dedication ceremony at the newly restored York Town Hall, in words that could apply to the town of York itself: "To the young, I would especially appeal — to you of the rising generation. Never suffer this house, which we this evening dedicate, to go to decay! Make it your purpose and determination to keep it always in good repair . . . We give it to you in charge as a sacred trust. See to it that no ruthless vandal hand defaces or injures it. Consider it a legacy given you by your ancestors and, I pray you, bring no disgrace on their memory by suffering it to go to decay . . ."

These words set an apt standard of judgment, for York's citizens and its visitors and well-wishers alike.